India's Women: Domestic Violence and Condom Acceptability in India

The Perspective of Married Women in the Slums of Mumbai

Dr. Rachna Walia Talwar

(Adapted from the Dissertation of the University of St. Gallen, to obtain the title of Doctor of Social Sciences, which was awarded to the author in September 2013)

2

Domestic Violence and Condom Acceptability in India:

The Perspective of Married Women in the Slums of Mumbai

DISSERTATION

of the University of St. Gallen,

School of Management,

Economics, Law, Social Sciences

and International Affairs

to obtain the title of

Doctor of Social Sciences

submitted by

Rachna Walia Talwar

from

India

Approved on the application of

Prof. James W. Davis, PhD

and

Prof. Dr. Miriam Meckel

Dissertation no. 4122

Acknowledgements

To Divine Providence,

Whose Blessings make everything possible

Lord, Thank You for Your Priceless Blessings

I would firstly like to express my deep gratitude to Prof. Dr. James W Davis for accepting the role of being my supervisor for this dissertation, for his valuable inputs that helped shape it from a research interest to a well defined dissertation that is presented here. I am also very grateful to him for his invaluable guidance, advice and patience. I would also like to thank Prof. Dr. Miriam Meckel for co supervising my project and for her confidence in this project.

Many thanks to the Swiss Government for granting me a scholarship to complete this research. Without this grant, it would have been very difficult for me to conduct the field research and pursue my objective of finishing this dissertation.

This dissertation is strongly founded on ground based evidence. For this I would first of all like to thank and express deep appreciation for Mr. Mayank Agarwal, Joint Director-IEC, NACO, Mr. Alankar Malviya, National Program Officer, UNAIDS, Mr Harish Sadhani, the founder and Honorary secretary of the first men's organization intervening against GBV, MAVA (Men against violence and abuse) for their valuable insights and inputs, which greatly helped me in the design of the questionnaire.

I would also like to thank the Dean of Lokmanya Tilak Municipal General Hospital and Lokmanya Tilak Municipal Medical College, Sion- Mumbai, for granting me permission to conduct the interviews in the hospital gynecological ward premises and am very grateful to the hospital staff for providing and ensuring a conducive environment for conducting the interviews.

This research is based on strong and rich qualitative data. While I cannot list their names because of confidentiality, I would like to thank all the research interviewees for sharing their innermost personal thoughts and opinions and experiences on some very sensitive and even some emotional topics in question, with me. Thank you all for your putting your faith in this research and your deeply appreciated inputs that made this research worthwhile. I would also like to thank those who made my field research convenient and safe. Thanks to Mr. Mahesh, who drove me all across Mumbai and being familiar with the local population guided me in the initial phases of field research to understand and become familiar with the population from which I was later to derive the study sample.

Also I would like to thank my in-laws, for their immense support during the field research and taking care of me like their own daughter.

To my parents and grandparents, for their constant support, encouragement, nurturing and blessings that kept me going all these years.

To my friend Eric Patry who has been my guiding star. I am blessed to have you as my friend.

Deep heartfelt thanks to my friend Nadine Khan, who took care of my daughter as a mother, while I was finalizing this dissertation.

Most of all I would like to thank one person without whom I could never have been able to finish this research properly and on time. I am very thankful to my loving husband, Manish Talwar for his constant moral support all these years, for being my Best friend, a friend I never had. I am immensely grateful for the sacrifices that you have made for me (the weekends and long sleepless nights and early mornings) to make sure that I am able to finish my dissertation properly and rapidly. "You Are the Wind Beneath my Wings" and I am so grateful to have you as my husband and best friend.

To my lovely 2 years old daughter, Roshni, who wonders why I am all the time in front of my computer and who has had to play on her own sometimes so that mama could finish her work. I Love you so much Roshni, thank you for bringing so much light and joy in my life. God Bless You!

I also thank everybody who contributed in any way to make this research study possible.

Thank you

Rachna

Ebikon, March, 2012

Table of Contents

List of Tables

List of Abbreviations

AIDS   Acquired Immuno Deficiency Syndrome

BSS   Behavioural Surveillance Survey

CEDAW   Committee on the Elimination of Discrimination against Women

CSW   Commercial Sex Worker

DV   Domestic Violence

DHS   Demographic Health Survey

EE   Entertainment Education

GBV   Gender based violence

HIV   Human Immunodeficiency Virus

HRG   High-Risk Group

IDU   Injecting Drug Users

IEC   Information, Education and Communication

MSM   Men who have Sex with Men

NACO   National AIDS Control Organization

NACP   National AIDS Control Program

NHFS   National Health Family Survey

PLWHA	People living with HIV/AIDS
PO	Protection Officer
PWDVA 2005	Protection of Women from Domestic Violence Act
STDs	Sexually Transmitted Diseases
STI	Sexually Transmitted Infection
UN	United Nations
UNAIDS	Joint United Nations Programme on HIV/AIDS
UNDP	United Nations Development Programme
UNFPA	United Nations Population Fund
UNGASS on HIV/AIDS	United Nations General Assembly Special Session
UNIFEM	United Nations Development Fund for Women
VAW	Violence against Women
WHO	World Health Organisation

Executive Summary

Background: With a population of 1.21 billion in 2011, India is one of the largest nations on the planet based on population. Yet the country has been fighting the AIDS epidemic incessantly for over two decades, since the first case of HIV/AIDS was discovered in 1986. There are estimated to be around 2.39 million people living with HIV in India. Today, the Indian pandemic has a new face - high seroprevalence among married women. One out of every three people living with HIV in India is a woman. With over 586 million women living in India, this poses an enormous risk to society. Almost 90 % of HIV Positive women have been infected by their husbands.

Objectives and Focus of the Research: This research focuses on low income, married women in India and their views on a specific set of issues considered exceptionally private: domestic marital violence, sexual and reproductive health, condom use. The study also explores their levels of knowledge about the above topics as well as self-empowerment and community support. The group under study involves married women living in and around an urban slum in Mumbai.

Methods: Qualitative interviews were conducted with the group under study: - married women in India from the low income demographic. A number of experts from agencies such as UNAIDS and NACO as well as doctors working with HIV patients provided expert interviews. The study also draws on previous studies and includes a quantitative survey, all of which are employed in the interpretation of the study's findings. The researcher adhered to guidelines on ethical principles developed by WHO and others while conducting her research.

Findings: The research findings showed that Indian married women favored their husbands over themselves in their beliefs and attitudes toward domestic marital violence. Strongly influencing their opinions were factors such as shame or the silent tolerance of abuse for their children's sake. The findings from this study also revealed that married women's awareness and knowledge about the legal support system was negligible. Although condoms can serve to protect against STDs and HIV/AIDS transmission as well as serve as an effective form of contraception, the findings of the study revealed that one of the major reasons for condoms not being acceptable to the women is because of its negative association with infection, promiscuity and lack of trust within relationshipThe study also revealed that condoms were not used as contraceptives for two reasons: the desire to conceive or completion of the family with subsequent sterilization.

Conclusion: Understanding the individual perspectives of the study group led us to conclude that even if all relevant information is available and/or accessed by women, it may prove insufficient if women's underlying attitudes and beliefs do not support women themselves in the fight against domestic violence, including sexual violence. In regard to condom acceptance, intervention programs should also address the need to dissociate the condom's negative image from promiscuity and disease and to promote it healthy means of family planning as well as AIDS prevention.

Executive Summary

Hintergrund: Mit einer Bevölkerungszahl von 1,21 Mrd. im Jahr 2011 ist Indien eine der grössten Nationen der Welt. Doch seit der erste Fall von HIV/AIDS im Jahr 1986 entdeckt wurde, kämpft das Land unaufhörlich gegen die AIDS-Epidemie an. Schätzungen zufolge sind rund 2,39 Millionen Menschen in Indien HIV-positiv. Die Pandemie wird heute durch eine hohe Seroprävalenz unter den verheirateten Frauen von Indien geprägt. 1 von drei Personen mit HIV in Indien ist weiblich. Dies birgt ein erhebliches Risiko, da mehr als 586 Millionen Frauen in Indien leben. Fast 90% der HIV-positiven Frauen wurden von ihren Ehemännern angesteckt.

Ziele und Fokus der Forschung: Diese Forschung ist ein Versuch, den von dieser stillen demografischen Entwicklung betroffenen Personen eine Stimme zu verleihen, ihre Ansichten zu den persönlichen und privaten Themen wie häusliche Gewalt in der Ehe und sexuelle und reproduktive Gesundheit bekannt zu machen. Diese Personen sind mit Problemen konfrontiert, und sie sollten durch ein verbessertes Bewusstsein, Wissen, Selbstermächtigung und Unterstützung durch die Gemeinschaft in die Lage gebracht werden, die Probleme zu lösen. Bei dieser Gruppe handelt es sich um die verheirateten Frauen aus Indien. Diese Studie konzentriert sich auf eine kleine Gruppe dieser verheirateten Frauen, die in und um einen indischen Slum in Mumbai leben.

Methodik: Mit der Zielgruppe dieser Studie – den verheirateten Frauen mit geringen Einkommen – wurden qualitative Interviews durchgeführt. Darüber hinaus wurden einige mit der Problematik vertraute Experten von Behörden wie der UNAIDS, NACO sowie Ärzte von HIV-Patienten interviewt. Frühere Studien sowie eine quantitative Befragung waren darüber hinaus wichtige Quellen. Die Forschung wurde gemäss den WHO-Leitlinien zu ethischen Prinzipien in der Forschung und anderen Leitlinien durchgeführt.

Ergebnisse: Die Ergebnisse der Untersuchung zeigen, dass indische Frauen die Überzeugungen und Einstellungen gegenüber der häuslichen Gewalt von ihren Ehemännern übernehmen. Die Einstellungen sind geprägt von Faktoren wie Scham oder stillschweigende Toleranz gegenüber dem Kinds-Missbrauch. Die Erkenntnisse aus dieser Studie zeigen auch, dass den verheirateten Frauen das Bewusstsein und das Wissen über die rechtliche Unterstützung fehlt. In Bezug auf den Schutz vor sexuell übertragbaren Krankheiten und HIV / AIDS, auch in Zusammenhang mit Empfängnisverhütung, zeigen die Ergebnisse der Studie, dass einer der Hauptgründe für die mangelhafte Verwendung von Kondomen deren Assoziation mit Infektion, Promiskuität und Mangel an Vertrauen in der Beziehung ist. In Bezug auf die Verhütung wurden Kondome insbesondere aus zwei Gründen nicht verwendet: Entweder wollten die Frauen schwanger werden, oder sie haben die Familienplanung abgeschlossen und entscheiden sich für die dauerhafte Sterilisation.

Fazit: Die verfolgte individuelle Perspektive auf die Personen der Zielgruppe lässt die Schlussfolgerung zu, dass eine umfassende Information nicht genügen kann, wenn die zugrundeliegenden Einstellungen der Frauen ihnen im Umgang mit häuslicher und sexueller Gewalt nicht helfen. In Bezug auf die Akzeptanz von Kondomen, sollten Interventionsprogramme auch die Notwendigkeit, das negative Bild von Kondomen zu bekämpfen, berücksichtigen. Es gilt das Kondom begrifflich von Promiskuität und Krankheit zu trennen und es als ein gesundes Mittel der Familienplanung sowie AIDS-Prävention zu fördern.

1. Research Objective

1.1 Introduction

India has been fighting the AIDS epidemic incessantly for over two decades; yet in the new millennium, it finds itself at a new battle front – the "feminization" (NACO 2006) of the pandemic. In the new millennium, while seroprevalence among the high- risk groups continues to be a significant threat, there is a new face of the epidemic emerging – high seroprevalence among married women in India (previously thought of as a comparatively low-risk group). One out of every three people living with HIV in India is a woman – almost 90 percent of HIV positive women have been infected by their husbands.

India occupies only 2.4 percent of the Earth's land area, but it is home to over 16 percent of the world's total population. In 2011, India had an estimated population of 1.21 billion. On a graver note, India accounts for over 75 percent of HIV/AIDS prevalence in South/South East Asia and approximately 6.7 percent of the global prevalence of HIV/AIDS.

It is estimated that India has an adult prevalence of 0.31 percent with 2.39 million Indian people living with HIV[12], which implies a

---

[1] While HIV prevalence is seen to be on the decline, it should also be noted that about 1.72 lakh (172,000) people died of AIDS- related causes in 2009 alone in India.

National AIDS Control Organization, HIV Estimations 2010- India, Annual report -

decline of almost 25 percent between 2001 and 2009. According to this new estimate, India ranks third globally after South Africa and Nigeria. It is however worth noting here that an even relatively minor increase in HIV infection rates in a country of more than one billion people could translate into large numbers of people becoming infected- e.g. even a mere 0.1percent, increases the number of people living with HIV by almost a million. While overall HIV incidence in India may be seen to have fallen in general over these last six years, one fact remains disturbingly unchanged – the percentage of Indian women has showed no decline; rather, it has remained constant at 38 percent.

Since the first case of the human immunodeficiency virus (HIV) in India was documented in 1986, there has been an explosive growth in HIV transmission. It has now spread to all the states and territories of the Indian sub continent. India's epidemic is as diverse as its culture. There is not just "one" single HIV epidemic in India but multiple HIV epidemics co-existing in different geographical settings and among different people with different types of risk. ~~While each region around the globe has its own particular pattern of~~ 2010-2011, P 5-6.

[2] "In 2007, NACO undertook an exercise, in consultation with Indian and international experts in HIV estimation, to revise the HIV official estimates based on the NFHS-3 household based estimates of HIV in the population age 15-49 years, estimates of HIV from the expanded sentinel surveillance system, and related information about HIV in high-risk groups that do not live in households. The revised HIV estimate of 2.47 million persons in India living with HIV (equivalent to 0.36 percent of the adult population) was released by NACO in July, 2007. **This national estimate reflects the availability of improved data rather than a substantial decrease in actual HIV prevalence in India.**"

National Family Health Survey (NFHS-3), 2005–06: India: Volume I, pp. 387.

the HIV/AIDS epidemic dominating that region, what makes India an interesting and highly complex case is that all these global trends exist here simultaneously, each having a high magnitude. Around the world there exist regionally dominant patterns – e.g. sex work (as in East Asia), injecting drug users (as in Eastern Europe & central Asia, Western Europe, North America and Australasia), men having sex with men (as in the Caribbean, Western Europe, North America and Australasia) and heterosexual sexual transmission (as in Sub-Saharan Africa). In India, such dominant patterns exist as sub epidemics in the different regions of the country. Even more interestingly, just as more than one type of epidemic trend may be observed at a regional /continental level around the world , so also a number of distinct epidemics in India often co-exist, sometimes within the same state, with different vulnerabilities, stages of maturity and impact. Nevertheless, according to Richard Fecham, the stakes reach far beyond India's borders- *"If we lose the fight in India, we lose the fight globally."*[3]

All possible routes of HIV transmission are known to exist in India; however sexual intercourse (87.1percent) is the most dominant mode of all.

Another aspect which makes the Indian scenario more dynamic is the interplay of contrasting elements- sexual morals and values are rapidly changing in Indian society, yet traditional gender stereotypes persist. With a GDP growth of more than 6 percent[4], India is one of

---

[3] Quoted in, Cohen, "HIV/AIDS in India." 2004.

[4] OCDE, India- GDP, Economic Survey of India 2011

the world's most booming economies. Although it is now the world's fourth largest economy in terms of purchasing power parity, 35 percent of its people live on $1 a day. It has emerged as a global player in information technology, business process outsourcing, telecommunications, and pharmaceuticals, yet almost half of India's women and one-fourth of men are illiterate. Stereotyped gender roles and sexual behavior create complex gender equations in sexuality which makes HIV prevention even more daunting.

"Although the epidemic differs from place to place, similar forces across the country aid and abet the spread of HIV, including strong taboos about discussing sex, the limited power that many women have and widespread discrimination against the infected..." (Cohen 2004).

The first case of HIV in India was reported among sex workers in Chennai in 1986. Initially, the epidemic was mainly concentrated among prostitutes and injecting drug users. The first half of the 1990s witnessed a rapid increase in seroprevalence among high-risk groups. According to a nationwide surveillance network, the seropositivity rate was noted to have increased from 2.5 per 1000 persons in 1986 to 11.2 per 1000 in 1992 (Lal 1994)[5].

In the mid-90s, expert studies strongly indicated that the virus was no longer confined to high-risk groups but was increasingly spreading to low-risk group populations, especially married women. In a study of women visiting STD clinics in Pune from 1993 to 1996,

---

[5] The author notes, however, that upto 90 % of the population groups screened thus far belonged to the high-risk groups.

the prevalence of HIV infection was observed to be 49.9 percent in FSWs and 13.6 percent in those who were not sex workers with majority reporting single sexual partner. This was the first evidence of high HIV prevalence among married monogamous women in India with a strong suggestion of risk from their husbands. Many other similar studies analyzing seroprevalence among married women in India acknowledged that single partner heterosexual sex with their husband was the major HIV risk factor for the majority of women and was inextricably linked to their husband's risky behavior[6]

.

In the new millennium, while seroprevalence among high-risk groups continues to pose a significant threat, there is a new face of the epidemic emerging – high seroprevalence among married women in India (previously thought of as a comparatively low-risk group).

As the epidemic continues to shift toward women and young people and is slowly moving beyond its initial concentration among sex workers, the rates of HIV infection among women in India have been rising steadily. According to NACO estimates, one in three persons living with HIV in India is a woman. This group constitutes 39 percent of all HIV infections, with 57 percent of these HIV-infected women residing in rural areas. Of these, only 0.5 percent of the women are sex workers. More than 90 percent of these women acquired HIV from their husbands or their intimate sexual partners. They are at increased risk for HIV not due to their own sexual

---

[6] "A number of small-scale studies reported that anywhere from 6 to 85 % of wives of HIV infected intravenous drug users and STI clinic patients were HIV positive." Hawkes and Santhya,, "Diverse realities." 2002.

behavior, but because their partners are men who are clients of FSW, MSM or IDU.

While infection was initially concentrated predominantly among sex workers and injecting drug users, it began spreading into segments of society not recognized as being at risk, such as wives who were monogamous, but whose spouses had contracted the virus from sex workers or other sex partners belonging to the bridge populations. Risky behavior by husbands has led to a sharp rise in HIV infection among married women in India. Married women who report monogamous sexual relationships with their husbands are a high-risk group for HIV infection in India (Gangakhedkar et al. 1997; Newman et al. 2000). This fact so boldly stated less than a decade ago still holds solid ground in the present. The latest national health survey clearly shows that HIV prevalence among women is closely related to their marital status. HIV prevalence is very low for women and men who have never been married (NHFS- 3 2007).

HIV/AIDS prevention policies in India face the challenge of addressing marital domestic violence, one of the starkest manifestations of gender inequality. Domestic violence is prevalent across all sections (regions & religious groups) of Indian society. Almost 40 percent of married women in India are victims of spousal physical, sexual or emotional violence (NFHS-3, 2007). Studies on gender and HIV/AIDS in India indicate that women in India may have an increased vulnerability to HIV infection due to domestic violence, sexual coercion, lack of control over sex, and lack of power to engage in condom negotiation. Not only do these studies highlight the impact of marital violence on women's vulnerability to HIV /AIDS, but also clearly indicate that intervention efforts may prove ineffective unless the issue of domestic violence is addressed.

The aim of this dissertation is twofold. Firstly, it attempts to understand the attitudes and beliefs of married Indian women toward tolerating marital physical and sexual violence and forced unsafe sex. Secondly, it further tries to explore reasons, other than violence, for low condom use within marriage.

While analyzing the social construct of gender in India, Dr. Suniti Solomon, who diagnosed the first case of HIV in India, notes that in addition to biological vulnerability:

"The lack of opportunities for young women to receive sex education and HIV information leads them to accumulate unverifiable myths. Social norms only encourage "innocent" women, e.g., who is sexually naive until marriage, does not seek pleasure from sex, one who would willingly and actively participate in sex only for the pleasure of her husband. Women's economic dependence on men causes poor health-seeking behaviors. Reproductive tract infections are not promptly treated increasing their susceptibility to HIV. Women with poor social and job skills feel inclined to offer sexual services or to offer sex in return for social support. These women are more likely to stay within a marriage no matter how vulnerable they are to infection. Motherhood, no doubt noble, also enslaves women. Fertility pressures force women to abandon caution when having sex with a known HIV-infected partner. Marriages are saved at the cost of HIV. Women are taught to accommodate and be resilient in the

27

face of violence. They pride in being able to live in the midst of violence. Violence directly enhances one's vulnerability to HIV. Submission to violence encourages men to engage in irrational and unchallenged behaviors such as having concurrent multiple partners. The impact of HIV on a woman is much greater than that on men. In most societies, women play the nurturing role, in predominant cases, naturally and voluntarily. However, when she is HIV infected, which may imply an infected partner, her burden doubles." (Solomon 2003)

It is also a well-known fact that domestic violence is an experience deeply embedded in social cultural norms. Norms and values determine power relations, form beliefs, shape attitudes toward sexuality, masculinity and feminity, etc., and from these differences emanate structural inequality, violence and vulnerability. While the sharp rise in HIV infection among Indian housewives with no risk behavior of their own is a strong indicator of gender inequalities (Solomon et al.1998), it points up even more strongly their lack of power to protect themselves from their husband's risky sexual behavior. Community gender norms tacitly sanction domestic violence, which interferes with properly adopting HIV-preventive behaviors. Given the choice between the immediate threat of violence and the relatively less apparent threat of HIV, women often resign themselves to sexual demands and indiscretions that may increase their risk of acquiring HIV (Go et al.2003), e.g. having sex without condoms to please men.

Married women's vulnerability to HIV/AIDS cannot be attributed entirely to domestic violence. Domestic violence plays a highly significant role in increasing women's risk of HIV infection (García-Moreno and Watts 2000; Dunkle et al 2004). However, it does not put all women at risk for HIV/AIDS, nor are all women who are subject to domestic violence vulnerable to HIV/AIDS. While the role of domestic violence in HIV/AIDS infection in Indian women is still under discussion, what is clear is that the consistent and correct use of condoms coupled with risk reduction education strategies, continues to play an important role in the reduction and prevention of HIV/AIDS transmission. This is particularly necessary in countries such as India, where HIV/AIDS has become a serious public health crisis (Roth, Krishnan, and Bunch 2001).

Given the increasing number of people being infected with HIV/AIDS, prevention and control of HIV has been a top priority of the Indian government for more than two decades. Raising awareness and knowledge about the prevention of HIV/AIDS, including condom use, has been one of the most revered key strategies of the National AIDS Control Program since its inception in 1992. In this regard, key priorities of the NACP have been to raise levels for risk and behavior change among the general population, especially young people and women, to enhance their knowledge about HIV/AIDS and to build behavioral skills to enhance prevention practices (NACO, 2005; NACO 2010-11). Condom promotion has been NACO's key objective since its inception. In the year 2009-2010 alone, it incurred an expenditure of around three hundred thousand US dollars and nine million USdollars on condom promotion and IEC, social mobilization and mainstreaming respectively (UNGASS 2010)[7].

"HIV infection is entirely preventable through awareness raising. Therefore, awareness raising about its occurrence and spread is very significant in protecting the people from the epidemic. It is for this reason that the National AIDS Control Programme lays maximum emphasis on the widespread reach of information, education and communication on HIV/AIDS prevention. Changing knowledge, attitudes and behaviour as a prevention strategy of HIV/AIDS thus is a key thrust area of the National AIDS Control Programme......"(NACP-III)

However, while according to NHFS-3 data, 87.6 percent of married women and 98.1 percent of married men know about condoms, knowledge about HIV/AIDS and its prevention through condom use is not universal and is, in fact, disappointingly low. Only 36 percent of women as compared to 70 percent of men know that condom use can help prevent HIV/AIDS (NHFS-3 2007). Condoms are used by only 5 percent of married couples, which is a serious risk given that marital status is closely related to HIV prevalence. HIV prevalence is very low for women and men who have never been married (NHFS-3 2007). We know that comprehensive knowledge about HIV/AIDS among women is extremely low. Though lack of knowledge is one of the significant factors, it does not fully explain the reason for low use of condoms among married couples. While studies have addressed men's attitudes toward using condoms in regular

---

[7] UNGASS, "Country Progress Report- India, 2010." Annex 1: National Funding Matrix, pp. 84.

relationships, data on married women's perceptions regarding condom use remains scanty. Having data on married women's attitudes toward condoms would help to identify and understand the factors, other than marital violence, that influence low condom use within an Indian marriage.

1.2 Practical Relevance and Research Gap

The United Nations (UN) collects data on attitudes among women toward domestic violence using household surveys in which women (and men, where applicable) are asked whether they think that a husband (or partner) is justified in hitting or beating his wife (or partner) under certain circumstances. Questions are addressed to all women/men aged 15–49, regardless of their marital status and experience of violence. Based on the UN update in January 2012, the chart below depicts part of the survey's results, among which are those for India.

Percentage of women aged 15-49 who think that a husband/partner is justified in hitting or beating his wife/partner under certain circumstances

Country or territory	Total 15-49	Place of residence		Wealth Index Quintile					Source
		Urban	Rural	Poorest	Second	Middle	Fourth	Richest	
Afghanistan	·	·	·	·	·	·	·	·	
Albania	30	18	39	49	38	30	22	10	DHS 2008-09
Algeria	68	63	75	80	75	69	65	53	MICS 2006
Andorra	·	·	·	·	·	·	·	·	
India	54	44	59	62	62	61	54	37	NFHS 2005-06
Indonesia	31	26	34	38	34	31	28	23	DHS 2007
Iran (Islamic Republic of)	·	·	·	·	·	·	·	·	
Iraq	59	54	70	·	·	·	·	·	MICS 2006
Ireland	·	·	·	·	·	·	·	·	

Source: UNICEF, 2012[8]

According to the data provided by UNICEF, almost half of women aged 15-49 years in developing countries think that a husband is justified in hitting/beating his wife under certain circumstances.

The Economist magazine also covered the above theme in its March 2012 issue with a chart entitled "Hitting Women"[9], which indicates that the issue of domestic violence is topical and is in the spotlight of the popular media as well (that the UN is interested is clear from the chart above and from the fact that it conducts its survey globally).

This shows that the Topic of Domestic Violence is both topical and is under the spotlight of the United Nations as well as other popular media.

---

[8] "Attitude towards Wife-beating"

[9] "Hitting Women"

The following observations are based on the literature review conducted by the author (see Chapter 2);

- Previous studies have addressed the issue of women's increased vulnerability to HIV/AIDS (including factors such as the unequal power in sexual relationships and their limited ability to negotiate condom use , which may also be a result of marital violence or fear of such violence)

- The existing literature captures men's attitude toward domestic violence, while working reports, such as the monitoring and evaluation report on n the Protection of Women from Domestic Violence Act, 2005 (made by the Lawyers Collective Women's Rights Initative), address the attitude and perceptions of legal service providers such as protection officers and the police towards domestic violence.

- However, an individual woman's perspective and her attitudes toward and beliefs regarding marital violence are lacking. The research at hand seeks to provide this missing information.

A multi-country study on domestic violence by the WHO (2005) clearly stipulates that in order to tackle this widely pervasive issue, we need to address attitudes and beliefs that perpetuate domestic violence. By "attitudes", is meant not only attitudes of the community at large, but also women's individual attitudes and beliefs, which may be driven by societal gender norms (García-Moreno et al. 2005), that have been understudied.

Changes in the community's attitude and in women's individual attitudes need to go hand in hand, as they do not exist in isolation from each other but rather, influence each other are symbiotic. The process of enhancing perceived self efficacy and capability among women requires strong societal and community support and hence the need for community interventions as well. However, women must be directly addressed because no intervention strategy focusing on issues directly affecting women's lives, e.g., domestic violence, can be successful as long as the primary beneficiaries of such programs or strategies – women themselves – are regarded as passive.

According to Bandura, people have a hand in shaping the course that their lives take, by influencing their own functioning and by selecting and altering their life's circumstances. Among the mechanisms of self influence, none is more central and pervasive than beliefs in one's ability to exercise control over one's functioning. This core belief is the foundation of human motivation and accomplishments (Bandura 1997 - cited in Bandura 2004)

Knowing and understanding women's attitudes toward the above-mentioned issues becomes imperative in the light of the complex relationship that domestic violence and HIV/AIDS share. These attitudes are the "submerged part of the iceberg" that need to be identified so that intervention programs are able to respond appropriately. This individual perspective as well as beliefs and attitudes toward marital violence represents, in the author's opinion, crucial information for the structuring and design of social measures

34

and programs undertaken to address these issues. Without this information, such measures cannot be fully successful and may fall short of their goal as they will lack a differentiated understanding of their target audience.

Furthermore, it is also necessary to understand women's individual viewpoint (including attitudes and beliefs) toward their own sexual rights, their vulnerability and toward condoms, one of the main preventive methods for STIs/STDs, especially HIV/AIDS as well as a proven method of contraception method.

Condoms were known and promoted as a contraceptive in India – family planning method of birth control – well before they were advocated as an effective preventive measure against STI/STDs. Condoms in India are popularly known by the brand name "Nirodh" used by the Government, a Sanskrit term which denotes "control". The Indian government family planning program promotes three temporary methods: the pill, IUDs, and condoms. Of these three methods, married women are most likely to know about the pill (87 percent) and men are most likely to know about condoms (93 percent). Over the last two decades, knowledge of condoms among married women has increased by only 18 percent, from 58 percent to 76 percent (NHFS-1, 2, 3). While knowledge of condoms has not reached some 30 percent of married women in India, almost 95 percent of married couples do not use them consistently. This is a very high number and represents a huge target market to be captured.

According to Al Ries and Trout (1986), *"Before you can position anything you must know where it is on the product ladder in the mind"*. This study also answers the question where do condoms stand on the product ladder in the minds of married women in India. In order to understand the (non) use of condom among married couples, it is equally important to get an insight into their contraceptive practices and their reasons behind the choices made by them.

The contraceptive choices that couples make or do not make, their reasons for making those choices, or more specifically, their choice of some other mode of contraception over a condom or their non use of contraceptives: Answers to these questions would help us to achieve a deeper understanding of the dynamics of sexual and reproductive health and would, in turn, reveal information that has thus far been unrevealed. The answers would also reveal barriers against condom usage in Indian marriages and might help to advance HIV/AIDS prevention in the domain of Indian marriage. The author seeks to answer these questions and increase understanding of the issues from a married woman's perspective.

It was observed by the author that:

- Most studies have pointed out the unequal gender equation which limits women's ability to negotiate condom use.

- However what we also need to know is what women think about condom use with their husbands. Do they feel the need to negotiate condom use? If not –why not? If no, what inhibits them from negotiating condom?

1.3 Research Question

This research seeks to find answers to two main questions:

- **What are the attitudes and beliefs of married Indian woman toward tolerating marital domestic violence?**

- **What is the acceptability and "felt need"of condom use among married Indian women as a means of contraception and as a preventive mechanism against STDs, including HIV/AIDS?**

R.Q1 What are the attitudes and beliefs of married Indian woman toward tolerating marital domestic violence?

Marital violence, while in itself a highly serious issue, also involves the issue of marital rape and forced sex. The main question thus goes beyond identifying the attitudes of women toward marital violence by seeking insight into women's perceptions of marital rape and coping with forced sex and forced unsafe sex. In order to understand the dynamics of the attitudes of the group under study, this question is further broken down into the following sub-questions:

- **What are the attitudes of married women toward tolerating physical and sexual violence by their husbands?**

- Do married women acknowledge forced sex by the husband as "marital rape"?

- What are the opinions of married women in terms of coping with:

    i. Forced sex

    ii. Forced unsafe sex

R.Q2 What is the acceptability and "felt need" regarding condom among married Indian women as a means of contraception and as a preventive mechanism against STDs, including HIV/AIDS?

Violence and fear of violence explain only a part of the non-use of condoms. What still requires investigation is why condoms are not widely used among married couples. Condoms are also an effective preventive mechanism for the spread of STDs including HIV/AIDS. Inspite of this fact, why is condom use not prevalent among married women?

This leads to the following sub-questions:

- **Is having knowledge about HIV/AIDS enough to motivate women to use condoms?**

- **What are married women's expectations regarding their sexual rights?**

- **What are their reasons for not using condoms?**

- **Why are condoms not the "preferred" choice of contraception among married women?**

1.4 Structure of the Dissertation

This thesis is comprised of 6 chapters:

Chapter 1: Research Objective: This chapter presents the research objective along with background on the topic. It states the practical relevance and the research gap. Finally, it discusses the research questions which the study aims to answer.

Chapter 2: Literature review: This chapter presents existing studies relevant to the topic of violence against women as well as studies on HIV/AIDS. It then presents the view from the field of practice, where it touches on solution-oriented work done for domestic violence (DV) and HIV in India. The chapter also identifies the research gap and provides a theoretical basis upon which the findings are examined.

Chapter 3: Research Methodology: In this chapter the methods chosen for data collection and explanations of the selection of those methods are presented. This study uses semi-structured in-depth interviews as the primary method for data generation, followed by a structured questionnaire for data validation. This chapter also presents the geographical location and socio-demographic characteristics of the research participants and discusses the ethical guidelines followed by the researcher while conducting the research.

Chapter 4: Findings from the Research Study: This chapter presents the results and findings on women's attitudes toward and beliefs about domestic marital violence - both physical and sexual. It also presents their perceptions of and views on condoms and their acceptability. This chapter is divided into three sections:

4.1 Findings on Marital Domestic Violence

4.2 Findings on Condoms and Barriers to Condom Acceptance amongst Married Couples

4.3 Findings on Communicating to Married Women about Marital Violence, HIV/AIDS and Condom Use

Chapter 5: Discussion: This chapter discusses the findings from the research (presented in Chapter 4) and interprets their meaning using the lens of the existing literature and prior studies. It also presents in greater detail those findings that are especially interesting or surprising.

Chapter 6: Conclusion, Limitations and Future Research Directions: This chapter summarizes the key issues and findings of the study. It also presents both the contributions of the study to the field and its limitations.The chapter concludes with suggestions for possible future research directions.

2 Literature review

2.1 Introduction

This study draws from the literature addressing the topic of domestic violence and HIV/AIDS, mostly in the form of articles in leading health and social journals, as well as studies conducted by UN agencies such as UNDP, UNIFEM, and WHO. Given that the key focus is Indian married women, this chapter first provides a holistic overview of the literature in the field of DV and HIV/AIDS, followed by a discussion of studies on the issue in India. In this context, it firstly provides a chronological evolution of the nature of the studies done to highlight Indian women's vulnerability to HIV/AIDS and then explores the studies conducted in India more fully with an eye to the research objective, i.e., the study of the attitudes and perspectives of Indian married women toward both domestic marital violence and condoms. This review provides a conceptual grounding for the study as well as the theoretical framework to be used for analysis and discussion in chapter 5.

2.2 Violence against women (VAW) and HIV/AIDS

Violence against women has been recognized at the international level as one of the gravest forms of human rights violations. Thanks to early initiatives that began in mid- 1970s and early 1980s[10], the

[10] United Nations Decade for Women (1975 -1985); The World Plan of Action for Women, adopted in 1975 at the World Conference of the International Women's Year

41

issue had gained much needed attention by the early 1990s and in 1993 was recognized for the first time as a violation of women's human rights at the Vienna World Conference on Human Right. This was followed by the adoption of the Declaration on the Elimination of Violence against Women by the General Assembly.

The Declaration states that violence against women is "a manifestation of historically unequal power relations between men and women, which have led to domination over and discrimination against women by men and to the prevention of the full advancement of women"[11].

Definition of violence against women[12]

"Violence against women" means any act of gender-based violence that results in, or is likely to result in, physical, sexual or psychological harm or suffering to women, including threats of such acts, coercion or arbitrary deprivation of liberty, whether occurring in public or in private life.

Violence against women shall be understood to encompass, but not be limited to, the following:

(a) Physical, sexual and psychological violence occurring in the family, including battering, sexual abuse of female children in the

in Mexico City; The 1980 Copenhagen mid -decade Second World Conference of the United Nations Decade for Women; Third World Conference on Women , 1985, Nairobi

[11] A/RES/48/104 - Declaration on the Elimination of Violence against Women

[12] Ibid, Article 1 and 2

household, dowry-related violence, marital rape, female genital mutilation and other traditional practices harmful to women, non-spousal violence and violence related to exploitation;

(b) Physical, sexual and psychological violence occurring within the general community, including rape, sexual abuse, sexual harassment and intimidation at work, in educational institutions and elsewhere, trafficking in women and forced prostitution;

(c) Physical, sexual and psychological violence perpetrated or condoned by the State, wherever it occurs.

Over the past decade, some of the most groundbreaking research has been done in identifying and exposing the intersecting patterns and associations between gender- based violence and HIV. HIV/AIDS has been recognized as a risk factor for gender- based violence. Violence is not only known to contribute to increased risk of HIV/AIDS infection among women but also to hamper HIV prevention strategies. Physical violence, the threat of physical

"Gender-based violence includes a host of harmful behaviors that are directed at women and girls because of their sex, including wife abuse, sexual assault, dowry-related murder, and marital rape, selective malnourishment of female children, forced prostitution, female genital mutilation, and sexual abuse of female children. Specifically, violence against women includes any act of verbal or physical force, coercion or life-threatening deprivation, directed at an individual woman or girl that causes physical or psychological harm, humiliation, or arbitrary deprivation of liberty and that perpetuates female subordination."(Heise , Pitanguy and Germain, "Violence against Women",47)

For further discussion of this problem, see Heise, Pitanguy and Germain, "Violence against Women." 1994.

violence, and sexual violence and coercion are all likely to be important factors associated with HIV transmission for women of all ages and in a range of settings (Garcia-Moreno and Watts 2000). The topic of gender- based violence is broad in scope and magnitude, incorporating a multitude of harmful behaviors[13]. The present research focuses mainly on domestic violence, which is one of the most pervasive forms of violence among women. A review of population-based studies from 48 countries from around the globe indicated that between 10 percent and 69 percent of women reported being physically abused by an intimate partner at some point in their lives ((Krug et al 2002), and between 10 percent and 30 percent reported they had experienced sexual violence by an intimate partner (WHO 2005).

Underscoring the link between violence and HIV in women, Zierler (1997) noted that women most likely to become infected are those who are also more likely to be with partners who threaten or use violence to control them. Empirical evidence shows domestic violence as a risk factor for HIV – through coerced sexual intercourse with an infected partner (Heise, Pitanguy, and Germain 1994; El Bassel et al.1998; Quigley M et al. 2000; Maman et al. 2000; Martin & Curtis 2004), by limiting women's ability to negotiate safe sexual behaviors (Kalichman et al. 1998; Davila, 2000, 2002; El-Bassel et al. 2000; Koenig et al. 2003, 2004; Karanja 2003) etc. Many studies have highlighted factors that mediate the overlapping of HIV/AIDS and domestic violence such as lack of autonomy (financial and/or sexual/reproductive), lack of communication, substance abuse, alcohol, forced sexual initiation, child marriage, low education, etc. However, it should be noted that most of these factors operate within the context of gender inequalities and power imbalances. While the findings on prevalence between intimate sexual partners may vary between studies from around the globe, they unfailingly point toward the fact that gender inequities act as a major catalyst that drives the epidemic among most women. Also, empirical evidence shows that gender inequality is the root cause of violence, which further increases their risk of HIV/AIDS infection (Garcia and Watts 2000; Kaye 2004; Dunkle et al. 2004).

2.3 Domestic violence (Physical & sexual violence) India

Domestic violence in India is becoming a topic of interest among social researchers and not without reason. It is being increasingly recognized as a social issue with serious health outcomes, including sexually transmitted infections. In the past two decades, there has been growing evidence from large and small community based studies (Rao, 1997; Martin, Amy Ong Tsui et al. 1999, 2002; Babu and Kar, 2009) as well as a small number of nationwide studies (Duvvury, Nayak, and Allendorf 2002; Hassan et al 2004; Jeyaseelan et al. 2007) that domestic violence is prevalent in all parts of India, whether urban or rural (Jejeebhoy 1998; Martin, Amy Ong Tsui et al. 1999, 2002; Roccha et al. 2009). The latest national health family survey (NHFS-3) recorded and reported domestic violence incidence rates at the national level for the first time. The national data shows that the magnitude of the problem (physical and sexual) within the subcontinent ranges from 6 percent in Himachal Pradesh to 59 percent in Bihar.

The data on sexual violence within the marital sphere is still limited. Though not exhaustive, various Indian quantitative studies (Martin, Kilgallen et al. 1999; INCLEN 2000; Kumar et al. 2002; Stephenson, Koenig, and Ahmed 2006) report sexual violence by husbands against their wives and are supported and elaborated by other qualitative studies (Khan et al. 1996; Rao 1997; Panchanadeswaran and Koverola 2005).

2.4   Studies on Domestic violence and HIV/AIDS in India

Citing three different studies from three different countries, a UNDP report (1992) acknowledged that for most women, the major risk factor for HIV infection is being married (Reid and Bailey 1992). One of the countries cited was India, and today, more than a decade later, the same holds true for India more than ever before. According to National AIDS Control Organization (NACO) estimates, one in three persons living with HIV/AIDS is a woman.

In the mid-1990s, on the one hand expert studies, mostly published in medical journals, revealed a new emerging face of HIV/AIDS in India AIDS - married women. At the same time, research in the social field brought to light dimensions that have been affecting the lives of married Indian women for decades - sexuality, gender inequality and domestic violence. It was only in the new millennium that patterns and linkages between these phenomena began to appear

46

more prominently in studies and there was a convergence between the two thus far disparate topics. Interestingly, George and Jaswal (1995) alluded to this linkage as early as 1995 in their paper on gender and sexuality.

In a study among women visiting STD clinics in Pune from 1993 to 1996, the prevalence of HIV infection was observed to be 49.9 percent in female sex workers (FSWs) and 13.6 percent in those who were not sex workers, the majority of whom reported a single sexual partner. This was the first evidence of a high HIV prevalence in married monogamous women in India, strongly suggesting risk from their husbands (Gangakhedkar et al. 1997). Many other similar studies analyzing seroprevalence among married women in India acknowledged that single partner heterosexual sex with their husband was the major HIV risk factor for the majority of women (Newmann et al. 2000) and was inextricably linked to their husband's risky behavior[14], which is indicative of stark gender inequalities. Parallel to these studies, research of a more social nature, by George and Jaswal (1995) has made an invaluable contribution in identifying the patterns of inequalities in the context of gender and sexuality (culture of silence, unequal power relations, e.g., women reported physical violence as a possible consequence of bringing up the subject of condoms or infidelity), that constrain women's ability to protect themselves from STIs and HIV/AIDS infection in India.

---

[14] For more information, see Hawkes and Santhya, "Diverse realities." 2002.

Among the varied studies on marital violence/ wife abuse in India, those by, for example, Martin et al., Go et al. and Silverman et al., in the past few years have provided valuable contributions to the existing literature. In their studies, Martin et al. not only provide empirical evidence of the high prevalence of spousal abuse, in particular sexual abuse (long underestimated) and consequent sexual reproductive vulnerability of abused wives, but also of associated factors which trigger violence. These and other very significant Indian studies have brought to light factors such as sexual risk behavior and poor sexual health and its positive correlation with domestic violence (Martin, Kilgallen et al. 1999; Verma and Collumbien 2003; Schensul et al. 2006) and acceptance of gender norms, violence and fear of violence (Go. et al, 2003; Bhattacharya G., 2004, Panchanadeswaran et al. 2007), all of which underscore women's increased vulnerability to and risk for HIV/AIDS infection and the greater challenges faced by prevention programs. Literature on sexual violence clearly points out that Indian women, especially those subject to sexual violence, are at increased risk of becoming infected with STIs including HIV/AIDS within marriage (Chandrasekaran et al. 2007; Weiss et al. 2008; Silverman et al. 2008; Decker et al. 2009; Gosh et al 2011). Women often submit to having sex with their infected husbands for fear of physical violence (Godbole and Mehendale 2005). Also, an increasing number of monogamous women are being infected. Given the limited premarital and extramarital sexual behavior among Indian women (NHFS-3– 2005-06), heterosexual transmission from husbands is the main source of infection for Indian wives (Gangakhedkar et al. 1997; Newmann et al. 2000; Mehta et al. 2006).

2.5 Attitudes toward and perception of domestic violence and condom acceptance in India

Studies conducted in India shed light on the following factors that can thwart HIV/AIDS intervention programs: poor awareness and knowledge about HIV/AIDS, attitudes toward and perceptions of sexuality, HIV/AIDS and domestic violence, domestic violence.(The last two points are discussed in the above sections [2.3 and 2.4]).

Let us examine each in detail.

2.5.1 Poor awareness and Knowledge about HIV/AIDS

Over the last ten years, surveys (large-scale surveys as well as community-based small-scale surveys) assessing women's awareness and knowledge have repeatedly shown a low level of awareness about HIV/AIDS and even poorer knowledge about its prevention and transmission. Despite a decade of "education campaigns about HIV/AIDS", only 57 percent of women who are or have been married have "heard about AIDS", and even a lower percentage (34 percent) know that consistent condom use can reduce the chances of getting HIV/AIDS (IIPS and Macro International - NHFS-3). In rural areas, this figure is even lower.

More than half of women in India are illiterate[15], which may be seen as an obvious reason for the low awareness level of HIV/AIDS.

[15] The literacy rate for females in India is 65.46%.

For more information, see CensusInfo India Dashboard, "Census of India, 2011".

However, more in-depth studies on gender and HIV in India find that, beneath the surface, married Indian women's poor knowledge about HIV/AIDS and behavior is in fact restricted by gendered norms (Padma Rama 2006). In India, as in many other traditional societies, sex is a taboo subject, shrouded in a culture of silence. Women in these societies are often expected to be ignorant about sex and passive in sexual interaction, which makes it difficult for them to be adequately informed about risk-reduction strategies. Even among women who are informed, unequal power within sexual relationships[16] reduces their likelihood of negotiating protection against disease, expressing their concerns about sexual fidelity, and saying "no" to sex (Gupta and Weiss 1993; George, Jaswal 1995; Gupta 2000; Gupta 2002; Pande et al 2011).

2.5.2 Attitudes and perceptions toward sexuality, HIV/AIDS and domestic violence

Beliefs, gender stereotype attitudes, shaped by traditional socio–cultural values, are one of the immediate barriers in adopting safer behaviors. In this regards, one of the first steps to changing a person's risky sexual behavior towards himself and his intimate partner should be to give up and change stereotype attitude in

[16] According to Perkins and Khan (2009), while among men the extent of state-level inequality may create conditions under which lower educated men engage in risky sexual behavior, whereas women may be less empowered to control their sexual behavior regardless of the inequality of the state in which they live. (Perkins, Khan and Subramanian, "Patterns and Distribution of HIV among Adult Men and Women in India", e5648)

regards to concepts like sexuality, gender roles and relation and concepts such as masculinity/feminity etc. Given below are two different research studies that help to justify this idea: One by Verma et al. (2006) and the second one is a DHS survey.

2.5.2.1 Verma et al. (2006)

According to this study, most young Indian men who reported partner violence supported inequitable gender norms. The research data also highlights the influence that masculinity holds over domains like sexuality, violence and disease prevention. For example:

- In regard to sexuality and sexual relationships, almost half (42 percent) of the male respondents agreed with the statement that "It is the man who decides what type of sex to have."
- In the violence domain, over a third (36 percent) agreed that "A woman should tolerate violence in order to keep her family together."
- Over half (55 percent) reported that "Women who carry condoms on them are easy".

While emphasizing the importance of challenging the views of masculinity to reduce young men's and women's vulnerability to HIV (Weiss, Whelan and Gupta 2000), other studies also note that it is equally essential to break stereotype gendered attitudes among women.

"...Cultural traditions pose obstacles to woman's health and flourishing. Depressingly, many traditions have portrayed women as

less important than men ... ... Sometimes these traditions are resisted by women themselves .Sometimes, on the other hand, they have become so deeply internalized that they seem to record what is 'right' and 'natural', and women themselves frequently come to endorse their second class status."[17]

2.5.2.2 Demographic and Health multiple country survey (Kishor and Johnson 2004)

Exploring the domestic violence-attitude relationship, this survey showed that in every country, rates of violence are higher for women who agree at all with wife beating than among women who do not agree with any reason.

As per the DHS survey, a large proportion of women in India (70%) believe that wife beating may be justified for reasons such as refusing to have sex or not preparing food on time. In every country surveyed, rates of violence are higher for women who agree at all that wife beating is justified, than among women who do not agree with any reason for justifying wife beating. As much as 80% more women experience violence when they agree with reasons for justifying wife beating, than women who don't agree with the same.

In India, women who agree with one or more reasons for refusing sex with their husbands (37-41 percent) are more likely to experience physical or sexual violence than women who do not agree with any

---

[17] Nussbaum and Glover. Women, culture, and development: A study of human capabilities. 1995.

reason for refusing sex (32 percent). Women who say that wife beating is justified for any of the seven reasons listed in the survey have a higher prevalence of all forms of violence than women who do not agree with any of the reasons indicated. For example, the prevalence of physical or sexual violence for women who agree with one or more reasons justifying a husband beating his wife is 41-44 percent, compared with 30 percent for women who do not agree with any reason (Kishor and Johnson 2004). These results are also considered to be compatible with the idea that gender norms reinforce inequality and violence in marital relationships.

As discussed above, studies on domestic violence within India have largely documented the magnitude of the problem, risk factors associated with DV, increased vulnerability of women to STDs, including HIV/AIDS. Also, community-based studies have explored the experience of domestic violence, including sexual violence within the marital setting, and shed light on individual, societal, and community-level determinants of DV.

However, previous studies surveyed and documented only attitudes of men in regard to domestic violence (Martin et al. 2002; Verma et al. 2006). Secondly, few Indian qualitiative studies in this area (e.g., Vivian F Go et al. 2003) have surveyed women, along with men. The study by Vivian F Go et al. (2003) however, focuses on factors which trigger and intensify domestic violence and also indicates the normative threshold of violence acceptability within marriage. In their two other studies, Go et al. (2003), and Sivaram et al.(2005) (though on smaller-scale) delved deeper into understanding how

53

social structure, community norms and relational factors influence the nature of violence while posing a greater challenge for AIDS prevention interventions. To the researcher's knowledge, no qualitative study has explicitly analyzed married women's attitudes towards domestic violence, including rape in marriage. Married women's tolerant attitudes toward violence, reflecting their acceptance of the submissive status of women and unequal gender roles, could present serious obstacles for socio-legal prevention programs to effectively tackle this widely pervasive problem but could also be detrimental to HIV prevention interventions. In this regard, one part of this dissertation aims to highlight some of the opinions and attitudes of married women toward physical abuse, sexual abuse, and marital rape as well as forced unsafe sex and also their perspective on seeking help in cases of forced unwanted sex and forced unsafe sex. The implications of findings on intervention programs are briefly discussed.

As mentioned above, many research studies in the area have highlighted barriers to HIV prevention among women in India, socio-cultural beliefs regarding HIV transmission, risk perception, structural barriers – gender inequality, which translates into low decision-making power –social as well as sexual, and more importantly, domestic and sexual violence, as precursors to non use of condoms. Research focusing on married women's vulnerability to domestic violence mostly reasons that gender norms do not confirm to open, healthy sexual communication. This leads to unequal gender power equation and women's limited ability to negotiate condom use which place them at risk of infection. The studies mentioned above have also clearly highlighted the effects of partner violence on condom use and married women's sexual negotiation ability. These factors clearly play a very strong role in defining and explaining women's vulnerability to HIV/AIDS.

Nevertheless, the existing literature is limited under two pretexts:

Firstly, while these factors are applicable to women who are subject to violence and /or constantly live under the shadow of violence, they may not be applicable to all women who may or may not be subject to domestic violence. While previous studies show that the fear of violence may still prevail in the minds of these married women, regardless of whether they would be subject to violence if they asked their husbands to use condom. However, the "why" question is still open. With the exception of a small number of qualitative studies (Go et al. 2003), to the researcher's knowledge, no qualitative study in India has examined why this fear of violence exists, that is, what might explain a woman's fear of asking her husband to use a condom? In their study on the impact of DV on women's vulnerability to HIV in the slums of Chennai (South India), Go et al. (2003) posit that the fear of violence inhibits women from negotiating condom use with their partners.

Secondly, while there is ample literature that discusses women's limitations due to violence, and fear of violence, there is hardly any that takes into account married women's perspectives on condom use. Also, while a few studies have successfully captured attitudes toward condom use, their main study group is men (Balaiah et al. 1999; Bryan, Fisher and Benziger 2000; Cornman et al. 2007). Those studies with mixed groups involve only a limited number of women (Sri Krishnan et al. 2007), while other study sample groups are high income, English speaking, with fewer women participants than men (Roth, Krishnan, and Bunch 2001). To the author's knowledge, there is no study revealing married women's attitudes toward condoms. Do married women want to use condom? Do they feel the need to use condoms? – If not, what are their reasons not wanting to use condoms?

Despite using a wide variety of communication channels to raise awareness, prevention efforts in most developing countries are deficient in two critical ways: first, programs fail to reach the majority of the women across all socio-economic strata who are infected with and/or affected by the disease; and secondly, interventions pay little attention to the broader social economic determinants of high-risk behavior and cultural contexts within which sexual behavior takes place (Gupta and Weiss 1993). This is true in the Indian context as well. IEC and awareness campaigns are one of the main pillars of NACO's prevention program in India, but its prevention messages have failed to reach the larger masses, in particular married women.

"HIV infection is entirely preventable through awareness raising. Therefore, awareness raising about its occurrence and spread is very significant in protecting the people from the epidemic. It is for this reason that the National AIDS Control Programme lays maximum emphasis on the widespread reach of information, education and communication on HIV/AIDS prevention. Changing

knowledge, attitudes and behaviour as a prevention strategy of HIV/AIDS thus is a key thrust area of the National AIDS Control Programme......"(NACP-III)[18]

According to NHFS-3 data, two in five women have not heard of AIDS. Knowledge of AIDS is higher among married men (80 percent) than currently married women (57 percent). Despite the efforts to increase public knowledge about the topic, knowledge about HIV/AIDS among women is increasing at a much slower rate than was hoped and is far from being universal.

Heightened awareness and knowledge of health risks are important preconditions for self-directed change. Unfortunately, information alone does not necessarily exert much influence on refractory health-impairing habits (Bandura 1990). Programs that disseminate information to the general public often do so partly to encourage appropriate changes in behavior. However, merely providing information is seldom enough to accomplish such changes[19]. Increasing knowledge and raising awareness about HIV/AIDS represent only a first step toward the adoption of safe sex and condom use. The provision of information also does not automatically translate into attitude or behavior change, i.e., people adopting safer sex practices and using condoms in their daily sex life. If that were so, more than half of Indian men and women who

[18] "Awareness raising – NACP-III".

[19] Rogers'model of the innovation-decision process shows that knowledge is only the first stage of the process. An individual has to pass from first knowledge of an innovation, to forming an attitude toward the innovation, to a decision to adopt or reject, to implementation of the new idea, and to confirmation of this decision. (Rogers, "Diffusion of innovations." 2003: 168-218.

know about HIV and how to prevent it would actually be using condoms. While 36 percent of women and 70 percent of men know that condom use can help prevent HIV/AIDS, condoms are used by only 5.2 percent of sexually active women and 7.9 percent of sexually active men, whether married or unmarried (NHFS-3).

In their critical assessment of theories used in communication for HIV/AIDS, Airhihenbuwa & Obregon (2000)   posit that decisions about HIV/AIDSs are based on cultural norms and emotions and may not follow any pre-established pattern of decision making. They support this argument by citing Freimuth (1992), who stated that knowledge is not a sufficient condition for behavior change. Raising knowledge rarely positively correlates with behavior, unless one really understands the target audience and why they are not listening or interested in listening to the messages intended for their own well being. While many people may be made aware (a number of times) of HIV/AIDS and may be informed that using condoms can help them to avoid infection through sexual contact; however, the meaningful questions revolves around whether they are listening, and if they are not, why not. Understanding the reasons behind individual resistance is very important in helping to break down some of the barriers so heavily cultivated by social and cultural environments.

2.6 View from Practice: Solution Oriented work for Domestic Violence (DV) and HIV in India

2.6.1 Domestic violence intervention: What has been done so far?

2.6.1.1 Communication Level

Domestic violence has been present in the Indian marital sphere for centuries and has been deeply embedded in the Indian families for so long that it has earned itself a normative status quo by perpetrating husbands, tolerant wives and by-stander families and community. Except for legal recourse, communication channels (in terms of Information Education Awareness (IEC)) have drawn little attention in the public sphere to the issue of domestic violence. HIV/AIDS, on the other hand, began being addressed at the multisectoral level, including massive aggressive IEC campaigns soon after soon after the initial cases in India were identified. Hence, there have been few interventions to fight this longstanding social problem and even

[20] "Is This Justice?" A multimedia campaign launched by Breakthrough to Reduce Stigma Against Women Living with HIV/AIDS.

[21] The campaign ran from February to April 2007 and included television (all major channels including Doordarshan - the National Channel, Star Network, Sony TV, Etv and NDTV.), print, radio, internet and mobile messaging. The campaign focused on the states of Uttar Pradesh, Karnataka and Maharashtra, which have a combined population of 315 million. According to Television Audience Measurement (TAM) and the National Readership Survey (NRS), the campaign reached over 34 million people through television, 29 million through print and 18 million through radio.

For more information on this, see Breakthrough, "Is This Justice? - Summary of Campaign Evaluation".

fewer to successfully address the causal relationship between domestic violence and HIV/AIDS.

"Is This Justice?"[20]

One such campaign to address the link between domestic violence and HIV/AIDS was "Is his Justice?[21] " Launched in 2007, this multimedia campaign aimed to bring public attention to the stigma and discrimination faced by women living with HIV/AIDS, most of whom have been infected by their husbands or male partners. The campaign demonstrated how an HIV-positive status, compounded by a husband's death, often leads to a loss of rights and consequent eviction of women from marital and natal homes. An end line evaluation[22] was conducted to assess the extent and impact of the campaign in terms of reach and to assess any positive shift in attitudes toward women living with AIDS (WLHA). The survey showed positive change in two indicators: a decrease (22 percent) in the number of people who feel it necessary for a woman to stay with her HIV-positive husband; a decrease (10 percent) in the number of people who blame a woman for not satisfying her husband sexually. The survey however saw an increase in negative attitudes pertaining to shame, blame and enacted stigma toward PLHA, specifically WLHA. After the campaign, the increase in negative attitudes toward WHLA was greater than the positive change.

Bell Bajaao (Ring the Bell) Campaign - "Bring Domestic violence to a halt"[23]

---

[22] Ibid

[23] "Bell Bajaao.", A multimedia campaign launched by Breakthrough against domestic

Based on the above-mentioned survey findings, Breakthrough resolved to feature only one broad media message about domestic violence, hence the campaign "Bell Bajao (Ring the Bell)"[24]. This campaign has been more successful, as the message given is clear and exhorts by-standers to act as a proxy agency[25] on behalf of victims of domestic violence. They can be anyone, neighbors, strangers, or boys playing in the courtyard, anyone who is a by-stander and witnesses an episode of domestic violence.

Supported by governmental agencies, the Indian Ministry of Women and Child Development[26]and inter-governmental agencies like UNIFEM, Bell Bajao was a campaign initiated and implemented by Breakthrough[27], which is a global human rights organization that

---

violence.

[24] Ibid

The campiaign has won several awards - Silver Lion, Cannes Film Festival (2010), Silver at the London International Advertising Awards (2010), Gold at Spikes Asia (2009, 2010) etc.

[25] *"In many speheres of life people do not have direct control over the social conditions and institutional practices that affect their everyday lives. Under these circumstances, they seek their well-being and valued outcomes through the excercise of Proxy agency."*(Bandura,"Social Cognitive theory in cultural context." 1994: P-270).

[26] The Ministry of Women and Child Development (MWCD) and the Government of India made investments of approximately $5 million USD allowing" Bell Bajao!" ads to broadcast widely on prime time national channels. For more information on this, see Case study "Breakthrough's Bell Bajao- - A Campaign to Bring Domestic Violence to a Halt!"

[27] Breakthrough works through offices in India and the United States on several issues including women's rights, sexuality and HIV/AIDS, racial justice, and immigrant rights.

uses the power of media for community mobilization. Launched in 2008, Bell Bajao calls on men and boys to take a stand against domestic violence (DV).

The ads show a man or a boy who hears a woman being beaten behind the closed door of her home. After a moment of deliberation, the man or boy then rings the doorbell of the woman's home. When the abuser comes to the door, the man or boy asks to borrow a cup of milk (in one ad) or use the phone or to retrieve a lost cricket ball (in others). From the ads, it is clear that the bell ringer is making the request as a pretext: He has heard violence committed against a woman and is putting the abuser on notice that the violence will not be tolerated.

The goal of the campaign was to advance the current discussion and knowledge about violence against women. Recognizing the significance of involving men as partners in its efforts against domestic violence, the campaign's main strategy was to address bystanders, reasoning that the campaign could engage bystanders to stop violence by appealing to their positive emotions of respect and love for women — as opposed to approaching them from the perspective of guilt or negative emotions stemming from inaction.

Both the media campaigns are very striking and inspirational, especially the second (Bell Bajao). However, the media has not yet recognized or addressed the increased vulnerability of married female victims of domestic violence (physical/sexual violence) to HIV/AIDS. The author would also like to point out here that while addressing by-standers is a very strategic and significant initial step,

62

it is essential, perhaps more essential, to use the power of communication to promote women's personal self efficacy[28]. Bandura notes that the exercise of personal control over sexual situations that carry the risk of infection calls for skills and self efficacy in communicating frankly about sexual matters and protective sexual methods and ensuring their use (Bandura 1994).

2.6.1.2 Legal Intervention /infrastructural level

One of the first and immediate efforts to help empower women was the implementation of the DV Act 2005. The bill relies on the UN framework for model legislation[29] on domestic violence, which mandates a broad and inclusive definition of domestic violence and states:

Art 11. All acts of gender-based physical, psychological and sexual abuse by a family member against women in the family, ranging from simple assaults to aggravated physical battery, kidnapping, threats, intimidation, coercion, stalking, humiliating verbal abuse, forcible or unlawful entry, arson, destruction of property, sexual violence, marital rape, dowry or bride-price related violence, female genital mutilation, violence related to exploitation through prostitution, violence against household workers and attempts to commit such acts shall be termed "domestic violence".

---

[28] Bandura, "Social cognitive theory for personal and social change by enabling media" 75-96.

[29] E/CN.4/1996/53/Add.2- A framework for model legislation on domestic violence

The PWDVA - Protection of Women from Domestic Violence Act (DV Act) 2005[30] was enacted with the objective of protecting women from all forms of domestic violence. In defining domestic violence, the Act went beyond mere physical forms of violence, to include mental, sexual and economic violence. In its written form, its distinctive feature is that it provides women with a civil remedy. It also prescribes strict penalties for the breach of protection orders. Moreover, the role of the protection officer (PO) as a primary link between the victim and the court is a significant step to embolden women to initiate legal action against the perpetrators.

However, since the enactment of the Act, there have appeared several gaps involving efficient infrastructure, without which the Act's implementation will be far from satisfactory. Without effective implementation, the Act's primary objective, i.e. to empower women to break their silence about violence, will be seriously jeopardized.

While this move has been widely appreciated, there are deep concerns about the absence of a comprehensive plan and mechanisms to effectively enforce the Act and address domestic violence. In the six years since the bill was passed, India has not yet sensitized public officials (especially law enforcement officials, the judiciary, health-care providers and social workers) to violence against women, including marital domestic violence. Weak law enforcement and the gender insensitivity of the various functionaries have failed to check the growing violence against women. At the same time, the extremely poor levels of awareness of women's rights

---

[30] "Protection of Women against Domestic Violence Act 2005"

among women themselves on their rights also perpetuate violence against them. The lack of adequate rehabilitation and reintegration facilities is another crucial factor that further victimizes women who have been victimized or ostracized by the community. These gaps have been observed and pointed out by the Lawyers Collective[31] in their fifth annual monitoring and evaluation report (2012) on the PWDA -2005[32].

Some of the principal gaps that have been highlighted by monitoring and evaluation reports are a lack of sufficient resources, inadequate coordination among the various stakeholders, lack of clarity on the role of police in the implementation of the PWDA, and more importantly, the changing mindset of the stakeholders in regard to domestic violence. Any degree of mobilization at the community or individual level however will be in vain if the safety net that battered women so direly need at the time they decide to seek external help is weak or absent. Debate regarding the magnitude of the problem is also clouded by the fact that domestic violence is a crime that is

[31] The Lawyers Collective is a group of lawyers with a mission to empower and change the status of marginalized groups through the effective use of law, and an engagement in human rights advocacy, legal aid and litigation. LCWRI actively uses the law as a tool to address critical issues of women such as domestic violence, sexual harassment at the workplace, matrimonial and family related matters, crimes against women particularly sexual assault and reproductive rights.

The LCWRI was instrumental in the drafting of, lobbying for and enactment of the Protection of Women from Domestic Violence Act, 2005 (PWDVA).

[32] "Staying Alive", Fourth Monitoring & Evaluation Report 2010 on the Protection of Women from Domestic Violence Act, 2005.

This Report was prepared in collaboration with The International Center for Research on Women (ICRW) and UN Trust Fund to End Violence against Women.

under-recorded and under-reported (UNICEF 2000). According to Heise et al. (Heise, Pitanguy, and Germain 1994), insensitive treatment of women and girls by police and the judiciary is one of the predominant factors perpetuating domestic violence. A bill alone is not enough to prevent domestic abuse; what is needed is a change in mindset (Kaur and Garg 2008). Studies suggest that the most successful interventions are those that combine a wide range of intersectoral and upstream approaches as well as downstream interventions. For example, interventions at the individual level to empower women to deal with violent threats to their mental and physical health are important. However, interventions are also needed at the structural level, where governments have a central role in policy and legislation and in mandating organizational change to ensure that women are in a position to be empowered (O"stlin et al. 2006) . Thus, an effective broad-based response to violence must be multi-sectoral, bringing together social, legal and health care services that address the immediate practical needs of women experiencing abuse and providing long-term follow-up and assistance, it must also address the normative and negative attitudes that encourage violence against women and undermine women's enjoyment of their full human rights and freedoms (Prasad 1999; Martin et al 2002; Kaur and Garg 2008).

The Lawyers Collective report it reveals that there is a strong need to establish co-ordination mechanisms between law enforcement authorities and public health officials on the one hand and, on the other, harmonization and implementation of gender policies and programs, especially in context of HIV/AIDS prevention. For instance, the insertion of a domestic violence component in NACO's training and gender sensitization programs and/or an HIV/AIDS component in various other non-NACO gender equality programs and policies could be a two-pronged strategy which would not only be efficient but also cost effective. The NACP phase three (2007-2011)[33] endeavors to mainstream gender-related issues in its programs by

-        Developing a gender strategy

-        Strengthening gender equity in programs

-        Reducing gender-based violence as an underlying cause of HIV

This is indeed the first significant step in recognizing a woman as an individual entity who needs to be protected and empowered. However, given that the correlation between HIV and domestic violence in India has only recently begun receiving attention, it will be some time before policies are able to address (effectively and efficiently) this nexus between HIV/AIDS and violence in the lives of married women.

2.6.2 HIV/AIDS Intervention – Promotion of Condom Use: What has been done so far?

2.6.2.1 National AIDS Control Organization (NACO) initiatives within the research context:

---

[33] Joint UN Support Plan for HIV and AIDS India (2007 - 2011)

Despite several awareness campaigns on a national level, NACO's prevention messages have failed to reach the larger masses, in particular married women[34]. Awareness and education efforts in India that have successfully reached other high-risk groups, including commercial sex workers (CSWs) and their clients, also need to target toward this often overlooked population (Mehta et al. 2006). However, the analysis of the IEC and awareness component of India's AIDS control program revealed that gender and sexuality have not been addressed in the design and delivery of prevention messages[35]. According to Amin, awareness messages in India mostly remain neutral in addressing the negative gender and sexual norms fuelling the epidemic. For Indian women, he further argues, most awareness programs scarcely address their risk and need for prevention information. He supports his argument with the following example: Awareness campaigns mainly target high-risk

---

[34] According to the latest NHFS survey, only 57% of women in India have heard about AIDS and only 34.7% of married women know that consistent condom use can reduce the chance of contracting HIV/AIDS (these proportions are even lower in rural areas). For more information on this, see International Institute for Population Sciences (IIPS) and Macro International, "HIV/AIDS Related Knoweldge, Attitudes, And Behaviour", Vol I.

[35] While NACO acknowledges that, the HIV epidemic has the potential to aggravate the socio-economic vulnerabilities of the "weakest" (including women) in society, and, the spread of HIV/AIDS is facilitated by human rights violations such as gender disparities etc. In this regards, it also admits that HIV/AIDS prevention and control strategies need to address the issue of human rights violations, in particular the vulnerabilities of women and children due to social, cultural norms etc. However, NACP (National AIDS Control Program) interventions have been mainly confined to raising awareness regarding HIV/AIDS, RTI/STD infections, VCT (Voluntary Counseling &Testing), care and support in context of the PTCT(Parent to Child Transmission).

For more information, see UNGASS India report 2010.

groups to promote and emphasize condom use when practicing high-risk behavior, but rarely insist that this group use condoms with their wives who remain *"uninformed, unaware and unprotected"*(Amin 2003)[36]. Research has consistently shown that an effective response to this epidemic will have to move beyond the supply of condoms, health messages for safe sex, etc., and start to address the social environment by tackling issues such as stigma, power/organizational networks and existing norms regarding gender and sexuality (Campbell and Mzaidume, 2002). Moreover, poor women in both rural and urban areas have limited exposure to mass media, and less formal education which also inhibits their access to information (Chatterjee 1999).

In 2002, NACO collaborated with the BBC World Service Trust (BBC WST), the Indian national television service- Doordarshan and the All India Radio (Indian national radio service) - launching India's first-ever one-year mass media campaign aimed at increasing awareness of HIV/AIDS. The project was named the BBC WST Partnership Campaign and was later extended for another five years. The campaign's messages were disseminated throughout India via a variety of entertainment formats, including television and radio. Some of the main features of the campaign were:

- Jasoos Vijay (Detective Vijay) &"Haath Se Hath Milaa"(Let's join hands): Telecast of a detective drama serial "Jasoos Vijay", a reality television show "Haath Se Hath Milaa" (Let's join hands), and eleven public service advertisement (spots). The main aims of

---

[36] Amin, "Comment - India's AIDS control programme".

the campaign were (1) to increase accurate knowledge about the modes of HIV transmission; (2) to increase knowledge about the means of preventing HIV infection; (3) to challenge the stigma of and discrimination against people living with HIV and AIDS; (4) Voluntary testing and counseling; (5) to promote condom use; (6) care and support treatment for people living with HIV and AIDS.

-**"Jo Bola Wohi Sikander"**[37] **(those who talk are winners)**: In 2006, the same partnership produced an award winning[38] public service advertising campaign, "Jo Bola Wohi Sikander" (those who talk are winners) to make condoms more acceptable across India. Over a period of two years, the BBC World Service Trust's condom campaign reached 150 million men across India[39] and intended to bring about improved attitudes toward condoms across a range of criteria:

• To decrease embarrassment in purchasing or carrying condoms

---

[37] "Condom is just another word."

[38] Ibid

The campaign received global recognition at the prestigious Cannes Lion 2009 International Advertising Festival. It won a Bronze Lion in the Media category and was a Finalist in the Direct Response category. The campaign also won an award at the Festival of Media, Valencia 2009.

[39] Ibid

Advertising on television, radio, cinema, print and outdoor media ran in four phases over two years nationally, with a focus on four high-HIV prevalent states: Andhra Pradesh, Karnataka, Maharashtra and Tamil Nadu.

- To decrease the fear of being negatively judged by friends or while purchasing condoms

- To increase interpersonal communication about condoms

The focus of the campaign was to get men to talk about condoms. Research shows that men who talk about sex are more likely to use condoms consistently.

The campaign positioned condoms as a product that men use to show they are responsible and care about themselves and their families. The campaign tagline communicated that "those who talk are winners" (in Hindi - Jo Bola Wohi Sikander), and "those who understand are winners" (Jo Samjha Wohi Sikander).

- **"What Kind of Man Are You?[40]"**: Breakthrough, an international human rights organization, has tried to highlight the fact that the majority of HIV/AIDS-infected women in India are married and monogamous and not, as popularly perceived, commercial sex workers.

The campaign titled "What Kind of Man Are You?", is an integrated communications campaign (TV, radio, print, internet, movie theaters, and transportation) in seven languages: Bengali, Hindi, English, Kannada, Tamil, Telugu and Marathi.

---

[40] "What Kind of Man Are You?"

- The Balbir Pasha[41] Campaign: Another campaign by the PSI (Population India International) /India called the Balbir Pasha[42] Campaign targeted men, encouraging them to use condoms. The campaign focused on the group most at risk—urban men ages 18-34 in lower socio-economic groups. It chose the group at highest risk, in this case urban men, because it believes that men can play a much stronger role in reducing the epidemic and that no single campaign can successfully address all groups.

PSI / India's campaign was designed to meet the following objectives:

- To increase the perception of HIV/AIDS risk from unprotected sex with non-regular partners by personalizing the message and creating empathy through identifiable real-life situations.

- To generate discussion about HIV/AIDS among the target populations and opinion leaders.

- To motivate people to access HIV/AIDS hotlines and voluntary counseling and testing (VCT) services.

After being launched with an initial teaser, the campaign unfolded and addressed three different themes:

---

[41] "Balbir Pasha Stirs Protection Talk." ; Prachi jatania,"Married and cheating? Balbir Pasha's watching you."

[42] Ibid

• The Alcohol Connection — "I often use condoms, but when I get drunk, I sometimes forget to use them." (Dec. 1-Dec. 20, 2002)

• Regular Partner Issue — "I only have sex with one person (sex worker or casual partner) and hence I am safe." (Dec. 21, 2002-Jan. 10, 2003)

• Asymptomatic Carrier Issue — "If a person looks healthy he/she must be safe from HIV/AIDS" (Jan. 11-Jan. 31, 2003)

Print ads, radio and television commercials and, most visibly, outdoor communication carried Balbir Pasha to locales and situations most frequently visited by the target group. Posters and billboards were plastered at bus stops, train stations, cinema halls and throughout the red light district. Interpersonal communication work, telephone hotline promotion and VCT services were endorsed on the ground to ensure saturation of behavior change messages from all possible angles.

Balbir Pasha Campaign

Significant Consumer Impact

PSI commissioned an independent research agency to conduct a post-campaign impact evaluation study with 1,500 people that showed the campaign messages were well received and effective:

• A quarter of all respondents recalled the Balbir Pasha campaign spontaneously, 62 percent recalled it after hearing "HIV/AIDS" and 90 percent remembered it after hearing "Balbir Pasha."

• Calls to PSI's Saadhan HIV/AIDS hotline jumped 250 percent and the types of queries changed from superficial to more substantive.

• More than a quarter of the participants knew the name of the hotline and over 75 percent believed that calling it would provide accurate and complete information.

• Retail sales of condoms in the red light district tripled after the launch of the campaign.

• The proportion of the target audience that has sex with CSWs and feels at high-risk for HIV in unprotected sex with a non-commercial partner increased from 17 percent to 43 percent.

• An increasing proportion believed that using condoms all the time reduces HIV/AIDS risk considerably (from 80 percent to 86 percent).

• An increasing proportion realized that using condoms half the time did not reduce risk at all (from 43 percent to 53 percent).

• Respondents showed an increase in risk perception regarding healthy-looking and more expensive CSWs and an increase in claims of condom use with CSWs.

Even though highly notable, this campaign in the researchers view still portrays the condom in a negative light, where a condom is something to be used only when having sex with a commercial sex worker. It has the undercurrent of being something which no self-respecting couple would want to use or no wife would want to suggest that her husband use as it could imply promiscuity and mistrust.

- **Red Ribbon Express (RRE)**[43]

The Red Ribbon Express (RRE) is the world's largest mass mobilization campaign on HIV and AIDS. Conceptualized by the national NGO Rajiv Gandhi Foundation, the campaign was implemented by NACO in collaboration with the Ministry of Railways, Ministry of Youth Affairs and UNICEF. Launched on World AIDS Day 2007, the train travelled across the length and breadth of India reaching 6.2 million people.

Through the Red Ribbon Express (RRE), NACO aims to:

- Break the silence surrounding the issue of HIV and AIDS by taking the messages on its prevention, care and support to people living in small towns and villages across the country.

- Create an environment free from the stigma and discrimination faced by people living with HIV so that they can access services without fear and prejudice and live a life of dignity.

Building upon the success of the first phase of the Red Ribbon Express project (2007-08), NACO launched the second phase of the project on 1st December 2009 to commemorate the World AIDS Day[44].   During the second phase of the project, services for HIV testing, treatment of STIs and general health check-ups were provided at halt stations. Mobile health units were deployed at many

[43] UNGASS, "Country Progress Report – India ", 2010, pp. 65

[44] Ibid

During its year long journey, the RRE traveled across 22 states, covering 152 halt stations.

halt stations. IEC exhibition vans and folk troupes have been deployed to carry messages into rural areas, particularly to reach out to those who are not able to come to the railway station.

Studies on HIV/AIDS related-information exposure and sexual health promotion in India are sparse. Those that exist, highlight the key role of communication using various networks in information dissemination. Continued large-scale campaigns using various forms of media including television serials, Indian movies, local media, and health camps are considered as one of the effective means of disseminating information among married women. These large-scale interventions show what a remarkable effort is being made in India to combat HIV/AIDS and are a significant part of the campaign, which has helped to reduce the number of Indian people living with HIV to 2.39 million. This 2009 figure represents a 25 percent decline from 2001. However, due to low condom usage among married couples and the increasing vulnerability of married women to HIV/AIDS through their husbands, it is important to understand the picture that condoms evoke in the minds of married women. Also, with increasing incidences of domestic marital violence, it is immensely important to explore the attitudes and beliefs and perspectives of married women in this regard. These topics have thus far been understudied and hence form a research gap which the researcher aims to fill through this research.

HIV prevention efforts are angled toward targeting groups practicing high-risk behaviors. While this is important, it is however not sufficient as married women need to be included in prevention efforts as well. The data generated from this research aims to aid in the practical application of prevention efforts to lower the incidence of HIV/AIDS cases among married women in India.

2.7 Conclusion

This chapter firstly provided a global overview of the literature addressing the issue of domestic violence and HIV. With India as its main focus, it explored the nature of studies conducted to address the two issues in question. It did so by providing a chronological evolution of studies done in the field: from recognizing monogamous married women at increased risk of HIV/AIDS, to understanding the socio- cultural factors such as unequal gender norms, norm-driven attitudes and perceptions toward sexuality, the unequal gender power equation, etc. marking this vulnerability. Furthermore, this chapter also explored within the existing literature attitudes and perception toward domestic violence and condom use as they are crucial to HIV prevention. Finally, it provided an overview of practice, including various interventions addressing the two issues. While exploring the themes addressed so far within the Indian marital context, with a significant bearing on this research, this chapter identified the research gaps that need to be filled in. The literature review provides the basis on which the perceptions and attitudes of married women toward marital violence (physical and sexual)[45] will be examined.

---

[45] Attitude towards domestic violence of any other nature –psychological, emotional, dowry related etc. are out of scope of this study and would not be explored in this study.

3 Research Methodology

3.1 Introduction

As discussed in Chapter one, this research examines the attitudes and perceptions of married women in the context of domestic marital violence and condom acceptability. In this respect, this research uses mixed method strategy to generate a rich data, which also includes narratives of married women in their own voice. The purpose of this chapter is to explain the choice of research strategy undertaken. It discusses the stages to the research process, including the qualitative method used for data collection and provides information regarding the research setting and location, as well as the socio-demographic characteristics of the research study group. Finally, it explains the design and source of questionnaires employed during the course of research. The methodological approach is discussed in line with the aim of this study.

3.2 Choice of Qualitative Methodology

The research strategy adopted by the researcher was to conduct qualitative interviews with the focus group of the study which was married women in India from the low income demographic. It also involved interviewing some experts on the topic from gencies like the UNAIDS, NACO and doctors working with HIV patients among others. Supporting the study with previous studies and a quantitative survey was a part of the research strategy.

A triangulated approach to qualitative data-gathering was taken to generate insights into domestic violence and to obtain knowledge and understandings of the dynamics of sexual and reproductive health as well as vulnerabilities to HIV and other STDs.

The researcher started the research by conducting Initial formative non standardized interviews (10 interviews) which were conducted in a slum in Delhi, (which was socially and demographically similar to the one in Mumbai). Along with these, 5 in-depth expert interviews were conducted in Delhi and Mumbai with experts from UNAIDS; NACO and a Doctor in Mumbai etc. After this In-depth individual interviews of 75 women were conducted at Sion Hospital which explored the dynamics between domestic violence and HIV risk. All the interviews were conducted after formal consent of the participant. All the interviews were audio recorded and transcribed by the author.

Described as, *"a conversation with a purpose" (Kahn & Cannell, 1957, P.149), in-depth interviews are face to face encounters between the researcher and informants directed towards understanding the informant's perspectives on their lives, experiences, or situations as expressed in their own words. The in depth interview is modeled after conversation between equals, rather than a question and answer exchange (Taylor & Bogdan), seeking deeper information, knowledge and understanding than is sought in surveys, informal interviewing or focus groups, for example* (Cited in - Holstein and Gubrium 1995).

In Parallel a standardized questionnaire was administered to 100 participants. One part of the questionnaire was used along with the in depth interviews for the purpose of cross checking for "internal consistency and reliability" of the interviewee responses and another part was finally administered after the completion of the first round of interviews to cross validate the findings.

Mixed methods designs can provide pragmatic advantages when exploring complex research questions. Linking qualitative and quantitative data not only enables confirmation or corroboration of each other, thereby offsetting each other's weakness but it expands the scope and breadth of a study while providing richer details and fresh insights (Greene, Caracelli and Graham 1989; Rossman and Wilson 1991– cited in Mile& Huberman 1994). In short, the qualitative data provide a deep understanding of survey responses, and statistical analysis can provide detailed assessment of patterns of responses.

3.3 Research setting and Sample

The selected research site in India was a low income, urban residential area in Mumbai – Sion and a slum called Dharavi in Mumbai and another slum in Delhi close to Daryaganj area. While in Delhi, the interviews were conducted in the houses of the

81

interviewees, in Mumbai, the research interviews were conducted at a Municipal General Hospital called Lokmanya Tilak Municipal General Hospital, locally known as "Sion Hospital", situated in Sion, a suburb of Mumbai.

3.4 Socio-Demographic Characteristics

In-Depth Interviews were conducted with 75 women. They were primarily living in the Sion area, the Mumbai Urban Slum – Dharavi, but were also coming from some other areas in Mumbai. The mean age was 25.4 years (range 19-36 years). All study participants were married. The average class to which the women were educated was the 7th class with 7 illiterate women, while only 2 had completed their graduation. They all belonged to the low income group. Most of them were housewives while some of them were doing low income jobs such as e.g. Domestic Helpers; Vegetable sellers etc. 62% of the interviewees belonged to the Hindu religion, while 30% were Muslim, 6% were Buddhists and 2% were Christian. The interview participants were randomly selected. 7 of them were HIV+ women.

3.5 Questionnaire

The questionnaire draws from the two DHS survey[46] modules;

- Woman's Status module mainly on three aspects: Woman's status module: WS 09 - decision making authority to earn money, contraceptive decision making; WS 11 - decision making authority whether to have a child; WS 30 – Opinion questions on certain aspects of family life (decision making, tolerating physical violence).

The researcher added some of her own opinion questions relative to the research (such as, woman's opinion on tolerating sexual violence, marital rape, wife's role in decision making about: contraception; sex; going to doctor in case of sexual reproductive health problem , how should she react to unwanted forced sex, forced unsafe sex etc.)

- DHS Domestic violence Module: DV 05 – Physical, sexual violence, DV 12, 13 – If her husband drinks alcohol and how often.

To the DHS module on domestic violence[47] where among others, questions such as

Q. Did your husband ever;

[46] MEASURE DHS – domestic violence module; women's status module, 2005.

[47] The questions pertaing to DHS Module on Domestic violence were deliberately kept in the end of the questionnaire , as these weresome of the most sensitive questions and the researcher wanted the participant to have opened up to some extent before she was able to reveal such information of sensitive nature.

- Physically force you to have sexual intercourse with him even when you did not want to? ,

Another question was added on unsafe forced sex by the researcher

- Physically force you to have sexual intercourse with him without condom even when you did not want to?

If the interviewee replied "No", the researcher added " if she unwillingly had sex with her husband in fear that he might get angry or violent" and "if she unwillingly had sex without condom with her husband in fear that he might get angry or violent, if she asked him to use one".

These questions were asked by the researcher to assess fear of violence among women that may prevent them from refusing sex or negotiating safe sex with their husbands.

The other part of the questionnaire was adapted from The Sexual Relationship Power Scale (SRPS) developed by Pulerwitz and Gortmaker et al. (2000). The SRPS measures power in sexual relationships and investigates the role of relationship power in sexual decision making and HIV risk. The SRPS contains two subscales that address two conceptual dimensions of relationship power: Relationship Control and Decision making Dominance. Among others, the scale includes questions about control over decision making, commitment to the relationship, condom negotiation ability, and freedom of action within the relationship. Most items use a four-point Likert scale, ranging from "strongly agree" to "strongly disagree." This study mainly employed namely Sexual Relationship

Power Scale (sub scales used - Relationship Control Subscale and Decision-Making Dominance Subscale. The main idea behind using this scale was to get a fairer insight into the women interviewee's marital sexual life to help the researcher prober deeper into relative issues during the qualitative interview, while at the same time ensuring reliability of what was being said by the interviewee.

The questionnaire was designed in such a way so as to get a better overview of the interview participant's martial family life, for instance decision making aspects in regards to their sexual and reproductive life. The aim of using the questionnaire was to complement the information given by the qualitative in depth interview, thereby obtain reliable and consistent data. The survey questions based on the DHS module, including opinion questions on decision making physical abuse, sexual abuse and marital rape, were then followed up more by more in depth opinion questions.

This Stakeholder analysis was one of the most important and imperative steps for this research, as on one hand it not only revealed attitudes, beliefs and perceptions of women and men regarding the issue, but also assessed their acceptance and perception of government's initiatives to address the issues (separately, like Domestic Violence act 2005, or together like NACO's programs in the field), and also identified communication gaps, potentially effective media tools and channels.

A second short questionnaire was designed and administered to 100 participants for the purpose of validating the information available from the follow up of the in-depth interviews. For instance, when

85

asked what should a women do / react if her husband forces her to have unsafe sex?, a series of answers such as remain silent, involve / not involve family members, or seek external support etc. came out of in-depth interviews with 74 participants. While the in-depth interviews helped get answers not only as to what they would a women do in such a circumstance, it also allowed the researcher to further probe deeper into the HOW and WHY part of their answers, getting to know more about their personal feelings about their own personal behavior if they themselves ever find themselves in a similar situation like unsafe sex and their reasons for reacting to a situation in the chosen manner. When the saturation set in the responses of the participants, the researcher then decided to validate the qualitative data by the quantitative questionnaire. For this, particular questions for example, multiple choice questions were made with 5 choices, what should a women do in case of forced unsafe sex: remain silent, seek help from family members, seek help from police, etc..

While conducting in-depth interviews, new questions and ideas came up during the researcher and interviewee discussion which needed quantitative backing to check their objectivity and validity. For instance, in one of the questions asked about their preferences to learn more about social issues and their solutions on televisions , a participant came up with innovative idea of holding talk shows on TV , as films are just a onetime watch, and talk shows has more to offer than serials. The researcher then included this point and developed a question:--to see how other women feel about it, before suggesting proposing the idea of talk show in this study.

3.6 Ethics

The researcher tried to adhere to guidelines on ethical principles developed by WHO[48][49] and others like The Council for International Organization of Medical Sciences[50] while conducting her research.

"Bearing witness: ethics in domestic violence research"
(Mary Ellsberg and Lori Heise)

"Epidemiological research on domestic violence, especially if poorly designed research could put women in violent relationships at substantial risk. Guidelines on ethical principals developed by WHO and the Council for International Organization of Medical Sciences provides guidance on the ethical principles of epidemiological research, including respect for people, non-malfeasance, beneficence, and justice. Main concerns of research include ensuring safety of respondents in a context in which many live with their abuser, protecting confidentiality when breaches could provoke an attack, and ensuring the interview process is affirming and does not cause distress. The inherent risks entailed in research can only be justified if the interview is used to provide information on available services and is a source of immediate

---

[48] Ellsberg and Heise. "Bearing witness: ethics in domestic violence research." 2002.

[49] "Putting women first:: Ethical and safety recommendation for research on domestic violence against women." WHO, 2003.

[50] "International Ethical Guidelines for Biomedical research", International Organizations of Medical Sciences (CIOMS); World Health Organization (WHO), 2002.

referral when necessary, if high-quality data are obtained, and if findings are used to raise awareness of, and improve services for, women who experience domestic violence."

The researcher feels very humbled to say that some of the interview participants gave a feedback to the researcher that they felt the interviews were very informative for them and at the same time very therapeutic for them. It allowed them to share some of their most intimate feelings and beliefs and attitudes towards very sensitive and personal topics for them which included sexual and reproductive health, HIV and domestic violence. Two of these persons were HIV positive women.

3.7 Conclusion

In this chapter, the researcher presented the methods chosen for data collection and the research reasons for the particular methods. This study uses Semi-structured in depth interviews as the primary method for data generation, followed by a structured questionnaire for data validation. Expert interviews and 10 in-depth interviews with married women were conducted in the initial research phase to obtain the view (on low condom use, HIV, domestic violence) from the practice and from the field, which helped in the design of the questionnaire. This chapter also presented the physical location and socio demographic characteristics of the research participants. In this chapter are also presented the ethical guidelines the researcher respected and followed during the course of the in-depth interviews.

Having outlined the research methodology employed in this study, the researcher, in the next chapters, will present and then discuss the findings on the perceptions and attitudes of married women in regards to tolerating domestic marital violence; condom use; and finally, the findings in the third section present the results of the questions regarding the knowledge gap and communication need of the married women.

4 Findings from the Research Study

4.1 Introduction

This chapter presents the findings about the Women's Attitudes and Beliefs towards Domestic Marital Violence - both physical and sexual. It also presents their views towards Condoms. This chapter is divided into three sections - in the first section the results and findings towards women's attitudes and beliefs regarding physical and sexual abuse including their opinions on marital rape and coping with forced (unsafe) sex, the second section addresses the barriers to condom acceptance amongst married women. In order to do so, it highlights firstly their expectations of sexual rights within marriage, explores their behaviour in regards to contraception and family planning, and their reasons for not using condoms as a preferred contraceptive. In the third Section are presented the results and findings in regards to the communication needs of married women and how they would like to be communicated to in regards to raising awareness towards topics such as Marital Violence, HIV/AIDS and condom use. It also speaks of their knowledge about legal support and other recourses which are available to them today.

As explored in Chapter 1, this is an important piece of information which would be necessary to have in order to address the issue of Domestic Violence and HIV vulnerability but which has so far been under studied. The objective of this research is to study 2 questions -

What are the attitudes and beliefs of married Indian woman towards tolerating marital domestic violence? And What is the acceptability and "felt need" of condoms among married Indian Women as a means of contraception and as a preventive mechanism against STDs including HIV/AIDS? This chapter is an attempt to answer these questions by means of the qualitative interviews and the survey conducted by the researcher.

4.2 Marital Domestic Violence

4.2.1 Results and findings - Women's attitude and Beliefs – physical abuse, sexual abuse, including forced unsafe sex

In this study, women were asked open and close ended questions; regarding their attitude towards tolerating physical and sexual abuse by the husband, and their beliefs as to how should they cope with it. Some of the beliefs and attitudes quoted below belong to women interviewees who have been subject to physical and or sexual violence at some point of their lives. There were 75 respondents.

4.2.1.1 Attitude - women's attitude towards physical and sexual violence

The opinion questions asked and their results showing women's attitude towards physical and sexual violence are as follows;

A) Physical violence -If a wife should tolerate being beaten by her husband in order to keep the family together

Table 4.1 Percentage distribution and narratives of married women according to their opinion , if a wife should tolerate being beaten by her husband

Agree – 55 (%)	Depends – 21(%)	Disagree – 24(%)
"It so happens that due to children the wife bears it quietly. It should not happen but it happens."	If he beats sometimes: *"No she should not bear it a lot, once or twice is ok but not always." (a DV Victim)*	"No, she should not bear it, in today's world at least not."
"She should bear it, only so much that it's ok but not a lot. R: How much should she bear? I: Only so much that people from outside do not come to know. Matter of the house should stay	*"When two people stay in a house there is friction. Like two pans when together make noise. Where there are no fights there is no love. People who love one another also fight sometimes. If this happens then it should be excused once or*	It's not necessary; the husband should be made to understand. If he is explained and he understands then it is ok. Means it's not necessary that she should live in the house after getting beaten by him. She should take the responsibility for her child and herself." (a victim of domestic violence – she claims it

92

Table 4.1 Percentage distribution and narratives of married women according to their opinion , if a wife should tolerate being beaten by her husband

Agree – 55 (%)	Depends – 21(%)	Disagree – 24(%)
in the house, it should not go out. R: why is that? I: Because my husband dislikes this a lot." *"She can take care of the children, she has her own house, she can live properly in her house, if her husband slaps her once or twice so she should bear it and sit quietly."* *"Sehna chahiye, are sahiga nahin to kidhar rahega"*	*twice. If it goes beyond limits then they should not live together. If it's only a little then they should compromise together."* If it is wife's mistake : *"If it's the wives mistake she should remain quiet. If it's not her mistake then why should she get beaten?"* *"If it is ones mistake then one can bear it."* *"If he hits without reason then it is*	is not every day just when they have a fight) "No she should not bear it, not hitting and beating. Nowadays a woman can also do some work and make a living. There is much work for a woman. She can do a lot. If the man hits and beats like this this has an effect even on the children. Small children when they see their mother being beaten get scared. So this must not happen. She can work by herself and also take care and feed her children."

Table 4.1 Percentage distribution and narratives of married women according to their opinion , if a wife should tolerate being beaten by her husband

Agree – 55 (%)	Depends – 21(%)	Disagree – 24(%)
One should bear it, if she will not bear it where will she live.	*wrong. One should not be quiet then. If he beats for some reason then it is ok.*	"She should not bear it because in today's day and age who will bear it. If she bears it will be torture for her only. Nowadays one should not bear it. The more she bears it the more the other person will put pressure and trouble more. This is the rule of the in laws house – the more you bear it the more they will trouble you."
	R: In what matters can one bear it?	
"kyonki shaadi ho gayi hai, apne ko woh kucch bhi bole , maare , bole, kucch bhi kare woh to phir sehna padega hai naa , shaadi ho gyai to mummy papa ke paas jaao, aisa to nahin naa, abhi woh jo bhi bole , yeh mat kar woh mat kar yeh to sun na hi padeaga naa	*I: For example when she makes a mistake, when husband says don't go here or don't go there and still the wife goes, if she lies and goes , then he sees her" and has suspicions about her. Due to such reasons.*	
	"If she is doing something wrong then she will have to live with the beatings.	

Table 4.1 Percentage distribution and narratives of married women according to their opinion , if a wife should tolerate being beaten by her husband

Agree – 55 (%)	Depends – 21(%)	Disagree – 24(%)

unka baat , abhi shaadi ki hai to ..pati kaa hi sunne kaa unke aage nahin jaane ka...

Because one is married, whatever the husband does, if he beats, shouts etc. she will have to bear it. Once she is married she cannot go back to her parent's right? Now if the husband days don't do this don't do that she will have to bear it. Now that she is

Even if that is me, I will have to live with the beatings.

R: Doing what wrong?

I: For example there are many women, who have some shortcomings in them, they make mistakes in cooking, they can't learn, they keep uncleanliness, and some don't treat their husband well, well husband is a husband right. When you respect him, then he will respect you. You can only clap with both hands, not with one hand only. If I will

Table 4.1 Percentage distribution and narratives of married women according to their opinion , if a wife should tolerate being beaten by her husband

Agree – 55 (%)	Depends – 21(%)	Disagree – 24(%)
married she must listen to her husband and not go against him.	*respect you then only will you respect me. (a DV Victim)*	

B) Sexual violence - A wife should tolerate being sexually abused
by her husband in order to keep the family together

Table 4.2 Percentage distribution and narratives of married women
according to their opinion that a wife should tolerate being sexually
abused by her husband

Agree 58%	Depends 5%	Disagree 37%
"One can tolerate for the sake of family and children ("pause....*Parivaar ki khaatir to dekho seh sakte hein..apne bacchon ki khaatir"*) *R: But should not tolerate being beaten? I: No* "*kya karein, kya karein, chup chaap to sehan hi karna padhta hai*" *What can one do, one has to bear it quietly. (a DV Victim)* *Yes one should bear it,*	*It's not really necessary. If she feels like it she will bear it, if she has some compulsions she will bear it. If she has no compulsion she will not bear it. R: What type of compulsions? I: For example if there are problems in her own parent's house, if she goes there she can't live there. If the parents are strong and that they can keep her, then she can fight*	*No its does not work like this, One should not bear it otherwise it will a torture right? In one way it's a form of torture. If she is not willing and he has drunk alcohol and come, has done something and come, and he forces her it will be against her wishes right?* "*No, it does not work like this. If he forces her .... She should love the husband a little, she should be*

97

Table 4.2 Percentage distribution and narratives of married women according to their opinion that a wife should tolerate being sexually abused by her husband

Agree 58%	Depends 5%	Disagree 37%
because he is the husband.	*with courage and she will not bear it necessarily. If in her trouble her parents can take care of her then she will not have so many problems. So it depends on this if one can bear it or cannot. (a DV victim)*	*careful with him a bit. She should explain him that you are a human being and not an animal. And if you have so much lust you can go outside. We will be common women, so one can't force us too much. You should not force us like this. You get good food right and you get to live comfortably – then you should explain your husband that you are a woman.*
The husband gives the wife everything so she should also give something back.		
One will have to bear it.		
(Victim sexual violence)		
"If she is one who keeps respect then she will bear it. If she will not keep respect she will tell her parents to help."		*R: in such a situation if he starts to go outside is it ok?*
DV victim		*I: no it is not.*
"It's an order from the		

Table 4.2 Percentage distribution and narratives of married women
according to their opinion that a wife should tolerate being sexually
abused by her husband

Agree 58%	Depends 5%	Disagree 37%
Divine. That she should bear it, so whatever he says she will have to bear it." *"If a wife has to live in that family in her in laws house, then for the sake of the respect of her parents she will have to bear it."* *DV Victim*		

As seen from the tables, majority of women are of the opinion that a wife should tolerate being physically abused (55 percent) and sexually abused (58 percent) by their husbands. The reasons varied from respect of the family and sake of the children to financial dependence on husband as well as financial condition of parents. Some of the interviewees admitted that the latter factor of parent's financial condition could be a point that most women would consider before seeking help from their parents. This is because they would be in better position to seek help from their parents only if the parents

99

were financially sound. In a contrary situation, most women victims of domestic violence, according to the interviewees, would have no choice but to tolerate abuse from their husbands. Nonetheless, for the sake of honor – of the self and that of the family as well as for the children's sake, were more weighty factors than financial dependence. This was true especially for those who agreed that the wife should tolerate sexual abuse.

Interestingly, an even bigger majority of women , including some of those who disagree that a women should tolerate being physically or sexually abused by husband, do not consider being forced to have sex by the husband as rape. This point has been discussed further below in the section on Beliefs of married women regarding marital rape.

"The Mother and father marry you off and send you – so it is his right."

For most of the women interviewed, physical, even sexual violence by husband is acceptable as they think that husband has complete right over his wife and can do anything he wants, beat his wife or force her to sex and it is for the wife to tolerate this abuse silently, especially for the sake of the children. Some of the women who agreed with this statement were themselves victims of domestic violence in real life.

"baraabar, iskeliye (for her daughter) main seh rahi hoon"

That's right; I am bearing it for my daughter's sake.

Few women partly agreed with the above two statements and based wife's tolerance to be acceptable under certain circumstances. For instance, it is acceptable to tolerate being beaten if a wife is "wrong". In NHFS -3 also, women agreed to certain similar reasons for which a wife should tolerate being beaten. Interestingly enough, it was noted in this study that some of the women partly agreed with being beaten or sexually abused if the frequency of abuse is within a threshold i.e. sometimes and not every day, or if a wife has certain compulsions *("majboori")* such as lack of a personal back up like parental support or any other safety nets to fall back on.

While a large majority of women (75 percent) agreed that a husband may beat his wife, almost none found it acceptable if a wife beats her husband, even if he is wrong.

- **Do you think a wife may beat her husband?**

I: No

R: What if the husband makes a mistake? (This Question was asked after the interviewee said that husband can beat his wife if she commits some mistake)

I: She can scold him, she can explain to him, but beating him is against the culture.

"No, how can she beat him? "

"A wife beating her husband (Shocked)? It is wrong".

"A wife cannot beat her husband; a husband can beat his wife."

Do you think a husband may beat his wife?

"That also does not work, but if a woman is wrong or does something wrong, then it's the husbands right that he can beat her.

"Yes Sure"

"If the wife makes a mistake and then the husband is beating her then it is ok but not without her making a mistake."

"Yes husband can but we people (wives) cannot."

"It's his right; he has married her and got her (laughs). In our people, the wife cannot speak; we cannot speak in front of the men in a raised voice."

4.2.1.2 Beliefs - sexual abuse, rape within marriage

Open ended questions were asked to 75 women interviewees in order to get some insight about their beliefs regarding marital rape and coping strategies, i.e. how they believed wives, who are being sexually abused, should react and cope with it.

(A) Wives' beliefs about marital rape

Marital rape is a serious social and Public health issue. With the exception of some significant research papers[51] throwing light on this problem from a socio-legal perspective, so far it has received little attention in India. To the researcher's knowledge, there has been no qualitative study in India which explicitly throws light on married women's opinions on acknowledging marital rape.

- ### Is forced sex by the husband rape?

To assess if women recognized rape within marriage, in an open and closed ended survey conducted by the author, they were asked if according to them a husband forcing his wife to sex is rape. Majority of women (66.67 percent) disagreed and denied it, stating that it is the husband's right and that a rape is one committed by a stranger not by the husband.[52]

---

[51] See, Ouattara, Sen, and Thomson, "Forced Marriage, Forced Sex: The Perils of Childhood for Girls." 1998; Waldner, Vaden-Goad, and Sikka. "Sexual Coercion in India: An Exploratory Analysis Using Demographic Variables."1999.

[52] In their comprehensive review on Marital rape, E.K. Martin et al. (2007) posit that the belief that women became their husbands' property after marriage led to marital rape exemptions, Sexual violence by a husband or intimate partner is often perceived to be less serious than stranger rape and is often not classified as rape (Frese, Moya, & Megias, 2004............). Marital rape is considered to be an extreme version of sex-role socialization due to concepts as "wifely duty," the belief that it is the wife's duty to sexually please her husband. It has also been noted that sex-role socialization fosters rape-supportive beliefs in both men and women (Monson, Langhinrichsen-Rohling, & Binderup, 2000............). See Martin, Taft, and Resick. "A review of marital rape." 2007.

As per the women interviewees, the husband has full and complete right over his wife after marriage which gives him the license to force his wife to have sex, whenever, howsoever and it is the wife's duty to go along with it in spite of her own will.

> *"When the husband is doing it, then he is in the right."*

> *"I: It's his right over the women. The women's rule will not happen...!*
>
> *R: Whose rule will not happen?*
>
> *I: A women's rule hardly happens. It's the man's! One day the marriage has happened then that's it. She has to adhere to the rules of the man with care. If she is happy then its ok, if she can't be then what's the use."*

Another reason for not acknowledging forced sex with wife as rape is because in their minds a rape is something that is committed by a stranger, who does not have the right over the woman he is physically forcing to sex. A husband, as per them, has complete

---

In an Indian study reporting extent of sexual coercion, "Milder forms of sexual coercion, then, may be ways of encouraging partners toperform their social duties (sex for procreation, marital stability) and may not be thought of as a violation of individual rights", not only is this social pressure acceptable within marriage, nor would it indicate a coercive partner. (Waldner, Vaden-Goad, and Sikka, "Sexual Coercion in India." 1999).

right over his wife's body and soul; hence his forcing his wife to sex cannot be considered a rape.

"No, No, how can it be rape! Rape means where I am sitting there someone else comes. This is rape. If they are husband and wife in front of people, even though they have problems and their hearts don't meet yet it happens. Now see in our case, Our marriage happened, I was 17 years old, I had no knowledge about my husband, that what it is , why is it, even though I had done SSC (Primary Schooling), but I had no knowledge of him, I was very small when I had been spoken for. But I did not know nor had I seen him, I saw him on the day of the marriage. Now in the start he is coming close to to me on the 1st day, on the 1st day he will use force, on the 1st day it will be his will which will be done (giggles), we have to be scared and do what he wants. "

"This is not rape. He is the husband is right, so he can do anything."

When asked if they had had sex anytime out of fear for their husbands 68 percent said yes, while only 11percent admitted that they had been forced to have sex. This could be seen as that these women don't let the situation get so bad that the husband needs to force them to have sex, out of fear they agree to it and this could also be the reason why they don't associate this with marital rape.

"If a husband does it then it is correct."

"I: The husband has the right over the woman; the woman's way will not work. R: Whose way will not work? I: A woman's way does not work; it is the man's way only. One day you have married then it's done, you have to behave properly with the husband. If you are happy then its ok, but you are not then what's the use?"

"No, No, how can it be rape. Rape means where I am sitting there someone else comes. This is rape. If they are husband and wife in front of people, even though they have problems and their hearts don't meet yet it happens."

"R: Did your husband ever force you to have sex ...? I: No, my husband never forced me to have sex. R: Did it sometimes happen that your husband wanted to have sex with you, but you did not want to and yet you had sex unwillingly thinking that he is the husband, you should not displease him, or that he may get angry /violent etc.? I: Yes it would happen like that , I would be tired , would not want

106

to have sex, still he would insist ...relentlessly... R: Did u ever refuse? I: I would refuse a lot, there would be fights as R: And then..? I: he would beat me, what else.... R: Then how would u cope. - tell someone or tolerate and give in... let's get it over with? I: Yes, would happen like that also, it would be like trying to get him off my back, means I would then give in to get it over with, I mean he would do it and it would be over. It would happen like this also."

One of them said they that one could call it forced sex but not rape. It is forced sex because it is just one-sided – only husband wants it, and wife has to do it in spite of her but it is not rape as he is the husband, who can do anything he wants, it is his right.

"I: See if it's forced, he wants to do it but she is reluctant, but the point comes to that only.

R: So is that rape I: One cannot say yes or say no, because he has the right over the woman, He has rights over her, but sometimes someone is not ready (is reluctant) because he forces one cannot agree either"

A few women (32 percent) believed that a husband forcing his wife to sex is rape.

"Yes from one point of view its rape only. Till a woman's heart is not in it, it is rape

R: So what you are saying is that in a marriage there can be rape

I: yes there can be.

4.2.1.3 Coping with forced sex:

The women interviewees were asked open ended questions regarding their opinion as to how should a wife react to unwanted forced sex and forced unsafe sex.

The following coping options were brought to light by the interviewees who were then quantitatively validated with a closed ended standardized questionnaire.

- **Unwanted sex**

Most of the women believed that a wife does not have an option but to tolerate sexual abuse silently, they might try to explain to their husband but eventually they feel a woman is at his mercy and if he still does not understand they feel that in such a case then a woman is helpless. Some of the interviewees said that they could ask for an adult intervention from the family, however, would go to the police only if they had support from the family, very few believed that one should go for an external support services such as police, as it brings nothing but more shame to them and their family.

The following ways to cope with sexual abuse came about during the in-depth interviews. They were then validated in the follow up short questionnaire administered to 100 women. Table 4.3 provides information of married women's opinions about coping and seeking help in case of unwanted sex.

a) **Tolerate silently; cannot do anything about it; feel that in such a situation a woman is helpless**

b) **Talk to adult in family**

c) **Call the police**

d) **Leave husband**

e) **Others (please specify)**

Table 4.3 Percentage distribution of married women according to their opinion to cope with unwanted sex

Tolerate silently	Talk to adult in family	Call the police	Leave husband	Others (please specify)

Table 4.3 Percentage distribution of married women according to their opinion to cope with unwanted sex

Tolerate silently	Talk to adult in family	Call the police	Leave husband	Others (please specify)
68%	27%	5%	0%	0%

As expected, majority of women prefer to tolerate being sexually abused by their husbands silently , than to talk about It in open, for they believe that it can bring shame to the family and themselves,

> *"Abhi aisi baat baahar jaake to bata nahin sakte , chup hi rehna chahiye na*

> *Now such a matter you can't go outside and tell anyone, you should stay silent only*

Also according to them "good wives" should not only keep silent, but should not let a situation go out of hand so that the husband does not have to force his wife, her will should be adapted to husband's will and desire. Since most women would not recognize forced sex within marriage, this could be the reasons that only 12% acknowledged being forced to sex by their husbands (*cf.* Table 4.6).

> *"kya maloom, abhi accha patni rahega to accha hi rahega kharaab patni rahega to kharaab hi rahega" R: Accha kaa*

kya matlab hota hai, accha patni kya karta hai? I:majboori se sona hi padega naa R: Aur kharaab patni kya karega? I: Woh nahin bolega naa, nahin soyega naa usme kya hai.

I: Who knows, now if the wife is good it will be good only, if she is bad it will be bad only.

R: What does a good wife mean? What does a good wife do?

I: Because of compulsions she will have sex

R: And what will a bad wife do?

I: She will say no and will not have sex. What's in that?

If both of them have an understanding then the husband will not do like this. Means if they have the same ideas then there cannot be force. If the husband has a desire the wife should agree, that the issue should not come to such a head that the husband has to force.

R: So what you are saying is that if the man has the desire, but the woman not, she should still agree and have sex? That she should understand?

I: One should understand each other's heart. If it is not like this then the husband will not be happy.

In order to keep their honour intact and also because of a much felt lack of social safety network, they believe that sealed lips are best for their own sake.

"Chup chaap rehne kaa.. Kis se karenge shikaayat..!

One should remain quiet. Who can one complain to?

- **Unsafe Sex**

The response by majority of women in case of unsafe sex was similar to forced unwanted sex. However unlike unwanted sex, more women said that they could talk to an adult in the family. Interestingly, majority women raised the concern that most would not know if the husband is infected and/or having clandestine relation. Given such a condition, they believed that instead of tolerating silently, a wife has the right to refuse or seek help from someone else. This may also be the reason or condition given by them to talk to an adult, else they could tolerate silently. Because in a normal situation not only do they trust their husbands completely, their risk perception to infection is also low. Table 4.4 provides information of married women's opinions about coping and seeking help in case of forced unsafe sex.

A) **Tolerate silently ; cannot do anything about it ; feel that in such a situation a woman is helpless**

B) Can talk to elders ,

C) Can talk to police

D) Leave Husband

Table 4.4 Percentage distribution of married women according to their opinion to cope with Forced Unsafe sex

Tolerate silently	Can talk to elders	Can talk to the police	Leave husband
51%	38%	7%	4%

4.2.2 Sexual abuse and condom use - fear of violence

In this study women were asked whether their husbands would get angry and / or violent if they asked them to use condom and why. Majority of women agreed that their husbands would get angry (99 percent) and / or violent (96 percent) if they asked them to use condom. Apart from the reason that husband could get angry if he wanted a child, most women admitted that their husbands would think that they do not trust him or would give their husband a reason to mistrust them.

> "I: Yes, he can get very angry. He will say "did I elope with you and bring you here, did I run away with you and bring you here, then why do you ask me to use a condom?"
>
> R: Why will he get angry? What do you think?
>
> I: He will say "Why did you say such a thing? Do I force myself on you? Do I forcefully say something to you, do

114

something to you? Do I do something wrong (go to CSW)?
Then why did you say like this to me? "That's why he will
get angry.

R: Is it right that he gets angry?

I: He will get angry then, he will feel that he never forced
himself on her, then he will get angry.

Some men's minds are like that, they get angry, is she
having suspicions on him, that he goes somewhere else?

He will feel that his wife is going to some other man that's
why she asks to use condom, or if the husband says they
should use a condom, then she will feel that the husband
was with another woman, that is why.

The data on fear of partner getting angry or violent if asked to use condom, was seen to be positively linked to mistrusting one's partner. It is this fear of springing up this negative association in their relation and consequently violence which might also make married women reluctant to negotiate condom use with their husbands. Table 4.5 provides comparative data (from the qualitative survey) on their assumption regarding husband's reaction to condom negotiation and their associating it with infidelity or mistrust.

Table 4.5 Percentage distribution of women who feel that their husbands would get angry/ violent if they asked them to use condom, and that their husbands could associate it with infidelity or mistrust

If I asked my partner to use a condom, he would get violent.	If I asked my partner to use a condom, he would get angry.	If I asked my partner to use a condom, he would think that I don't trust him.	If I asked my partner to use a condom, he would think I'm having sex with other people.
99%	96%	89%	82%

Finally, the participants were questioned regarding their personal experience (if any) of physical violence ; if they had been physically forced to sex by their husbands or were ever forced to sex without condom , even if they wanted to use one at the time of intercourse.

Table 4.6 Percentage distribution of women who were subject to physical marital violence, physically forced to have sex and forced to have unsafe sex

Question		Yes	No	Do Not Use Condoms
Have you been subjected to Physical Violence by your husband?		28	47	
(Hit, Slapped, Kicked etc.)	%	37	63	
Have you been physically forced to have sex by your husband?		9	66	
	%	12	88	
Have you had sex out of fear with your husband?		52	23	
(Husband may get angry or physically violent)	%	69	31	
Have you ever been forced to have sex		11	8	56

Table 4.6 Percentage distribution of women who were subject to physical marital violence, physically forced to have sex and forced to have unsafe sex

Question	Yes	No	Do Not Use Condoms
without a condom even if you wanted to use one?			
%	15	11	75

The results in the above table show that while 37 percent of the women admitted being subject to physical violence, only 12 percent reported being forced to have sex by their husbands. They were further asked if they ever had sex out of fear that their husbands may get angry, should they refuse. Interestingly, 69 percent reported unwanted sex, as they did not want to make their husbands angry and/or believed that even if the husbands may not have got violent on refusing them sex, they found did this out of an obligation /duty as a wife "should" do to please him. Furthermore, 15 percent reported being forced to have sex without condoms, while 75 percent were not using condoms at all whenever they had sex.

4.3 Condoms and Barriers to Condom Acceptance among Married Women

4.3.1 Married women`s expectations of her sexual rights in marriage

Many studies have highlighted the fact that Indian women have low decision making power when it comes to sex, especially negotiating condom use with their partners. In this study, two open ended questions were asked to assess as to how they perceive decision making in their personal sex life – this was further validated by the short questionnaire addressed to 100 participants the result of which is below:

- **Who should have more say in sex life such as whether to have sex or not, when to have sex etc.?**

- **Who should have more say whether to use condom or not? And, Why?**

Table 4.7 Percentage distribution of Who should have more say in sex and Who should have more say whether to use condom or not?

Who SHOULD have more say in sex life?	Who HAS more say about sex life in real?	Who SHOULD have more say whether to use condom or not?	Who HAS more say about condom use in real?
Husband -95%	Husband-90%	Husband -95%	Husband-91%
Wife – 1%	Wife-6%	Wife-1%	Wife- 3%
Both-4%	Both-4%	Both-4%	Both-6%

The results in the table show that;

1. 95 % of women prefer that husbands should have more "say" in sex life including whether to use condom or not.

I: It should be husbands decision after all he is the one to get it from outside- we women folk are not going outside to buy it, so it should be his decision if we should use a condom or not.

120

R: Normally this decision, whether or not to use a condom, who should take it? Normally should only the man take this decision?

I: No it is not like this, I can also take it, he can also take it, but whatever he says that will only be correct.

R: why is that? What does he know that you don't know?

I: If I have more knowledge I will take the decision, if he has more knowledge he will take the decision, that's how it is.

R: If today I give you knowledge and information about condoms will you be able to tell your husband?

I: Yes

R: What if your husband refuses to use a condom, what then?

I: I will try and convince him, that it is in our best interest and that we should use it.

R: And if he refuses then what?

I: Then it's his decision.

I: In my opinion the husband should understand, should buy it, he should use wisdom, otherwise the life can be destroyed, so that's why the husband should decide. However much the woman knows yet in front of her the man should use wisdom and should understand, she will not explain again and again to him ....(aurat maane kitna bhi jaanti hai lekin uske saamne aadmi ko samajhdaari se kaam lena chahiye baar baar thode hi samjaayegi aadmi ko.........)......

This preference that husband should decide whether to use condoms is however limited only to the extent that their health and well being is not being compromised with. The data from this survey also had similar results that majority (78 percent) of women would refuse unsafe sex, if husband is infected with an STD & or HIV/AIDS.

"If one has an option, then not without a condom."

I: It's very important for that to be explained. If the husband is with someone else, has sex with someone else, then he also gets infected and infects the wife as well,

R: in such a case what should the woman do?

I: She should stop him

R: How?

I: She should stop him, use a condom.

R: If he refuses to use a condom?

I: She should stop him; else she should take the help of elders.

If the wife knows then she should keep away, or else she should use a condom, it's the question of the whole life, it should be like this that the husband can be told, if he uses force, then in the future some action has to be taken about it.

However many women admitted that it would be possible for them to refuse unsafe sex with an infected partner only if they know about husband's STD /HIV Status (which remains mostly unknown).

"I: a wife hardly knows what he is doing outside R: But if a wife comes to know that the husband has a disease, is infected, but the husband still uses force and wants to have sex without a condom, in such a case what should the wife do? I: She should not bear it, should raise her voice against it."

"I: But we don't know where he is.

R: Eh?

I: Where do we know, how do we know if he has been to another woman and come.

R: If one knows then...?

I: then she can tell him to use a condom.

R: If the husband forces that he wants to have sex without a condom.

I: Then she can't do anything.

R: Should one take the help of someone?

I: Yes of course she should take the help.

R: Whose?

I: She should take the help of her in-laws.

R: Suppose the in-laws can't help can she go outside to the women's community or to the police?

I: Yes she can go.

R: Should she go?

I: No, No, she should not go, but if the in-laws don't listen then what can she do?

R: But if the in-laws can't help, even then she should not go outside for help?

I: No she should not go."

"I: But if one knows that (that husband goes out &/or he is infected) then only, the husband goes out the whole day for work, the wife thinks he has gone for work, if she knows otherwise she will do something for her safety., if she does not know then how can she come to know that he goes outside.

R: If she knows then what can she do?

I: Then she can speak in front of the husband, that you go outside and do like this, you can say anything if you know. "

They however mentioned their limitations in protecting themselves incase their husbands force them to unsafe sex *(cf.* coping with forced unsafe sex).

4.3.2 What do Interviewees say about using contraception?

Results

Majority of women were not using any contraceptive method at all. Less than 48 percent of the women (36 women out of the 75 Total respondents) reported use of a contraceptive method at the time of the in-depth interviews. The most commonly used method was female sterilization, used by 25 percent of all the women. Although only 9 percent and 8 percent of respondents reported the male condom and copper –T respectively as their current method; they are the most widely used of other temporary contraceptive methods such as pill, injection etc. and both are in extremely close competition with each other. Current use of natural family planning methods such as rhythm method or other traditional methods was not reported.

Table 4.8: Methods used by interviewees and their husbands

Copper-T	Injectibles	Pill	Condom	Female sterilisation	No method used	Total
6	2	2	7	19	39	75

4.3.2.1 Reasons for not choosing a temporary method

Of the 75 women interviewed 76 percent were not using a contraceptive method. Reasons for not using a method are broadly grouped as follows:

1. Most women (65 percent) indicated that they did not need to practice contraception. These women reported that they had reproductive reasons (were pregnant, wanted to conceive or waiting until after the birth of their first baby (22), were sterilized (19), or their husbands were infertile (2).)

2. 8 had not made any decision or even discussed

3. Reasons related to the method itself such as side effects, health concerns and inconvenience were given by 2 of the respondents.

4. Other two of the respondents reported reasons related to lack of knowledge about contraceptives.

5. Other reasons were given by 2 of the women. For instance, infrequent sex, 1 while others said that they didn't have a reason.

Most of the interviewees being in their reproductive prime were not using any contraceptive, let alone condom because they wanted to have a baby. It must be noted however that not all had made a conscious decision of making a baby or to not use a contraceptive for making one.   A lot of women interviewed have not had any discussion with their spouses about contraception, simply stating that neither they nor their husbands even thought or made any conscious decision about using contraception. Some of them have even had to take the risk of unwanted pregnancy and in some of the cases even abortion.

4.3.2.2 Condom as a Contraceptive

In the in-depth interviews, around 24 percent of women had not heard at all or had very little knowledge about condom, and of those who had heard, only around 7 percent of them were actually using it – 5 women out of 75. Those who knew about condom but were not using it gave varied reasons for not using condom which are discussed in the second part of this section.

4.3.2.3 Why is condom not as popular a contraceptive?

From In depth Interviews:

- Does not feel the need:

  - Using some other method; Switching to some other method; does not like it; inconvenient; fear of infection not on radar

  - Sterilized – want only contraception. Fear of infection not on radar

  - Want to have baby

Some of the main reasons for not using condom for contraception were that most of the women did not feel the need to use it for fertility reasons, like wanting to make a baby; others were already using some other contraceptive method, or were sterilized. Above all and most interestingly, majority women who knew about condom regarded it more as prevention against infection from HIV/AIDS, fear of which was nonexistent on their radar.

"If you have put Copper T then why should you use a condom, one who is infected with the disease will only use it."

"We did not want to do anything like that that we would need to use a condom"

"I: No, never used a condom, once we used it but it tore, I said I don't want it, and I don't even like it when I see it, I get disgusted.

R: but did your husband ever have a problem from using a condom?

I: Now if he uses it outside then I don't know.

R: Does he go outside?

I: maybe he does, he is a man. Men only go outside, from 24 hours, he is away from me for 12 hours, so I can't keep a tab on those 12 hours, where he went, why did he go there, when he went, when he came, all this I can't say, that he has gone outside somewhere or not, with me he used it only once, it tore and from then on, we did not use it, and later I got operated."

- Heard about it but does not know exactly what it is

- Does not like it (personal disgust, disposal issue, inconvenience)

Some of them expressed disgust for condom to the extent that they decided to switch to other mode of contraception.

"ghinn aise aati hai bhabhi ke aurat log bolte hein ke jab aurat log aadmi log judte hein, to sharer mein daal ke matlab ki kaam dhaam apna kar liya , kaam dhaam katam karke utaar ke baha diya, bacche log paate hein, usko munh mein leke phulaate hein, to aurat log jab yeh bolte hein to mugje to sunke hi ghinn aati hai..isiliye hum bhi jaan gaye hein key eh kharaab cheez hai".

"I feel disgusted, when the women say that after having sex when the condom is thrown away, little children find it and blow them up and when women say that this is what happens I feel disgusted just hearing it. That is why I have come to know that it's a bad thing."

"woh humko accha nahin lagta waise lagaana, waise lagaane kaa nahin accha lagta hai, woh bolta hai apna aadmi - apna ek khoon ek hi hai to aoun woh sab laga ke kya faayada hai bolta hai"

"I don't like to use it like that; my man says that we have one blood, why should we use something like that."

Two of the participants mentioned breakage, resulting in pregnancy and problem of disposal respectively as reasons for discontinuing its use.

"Nahin, condom kabhi istamaal nahin kiya, ek baar kiya tha who phat gaya tha, maine bola mujhe nahin chahiye, aur mujhe accha bhi nahin lagta dekhkar ghinn aati hai"

"No, never used a condom, one time we used it but it tore, I said I don't want it, now I don't even like it, I feel disgusted about it."

One of the main reasons for not like condom, thinking it to be dirty was because of condom's association with promiscuity and disease.

R: TV pe kya suna aapne? I: Yahi ke aadmi doosri aurat ke saath sambandh rakhte hein, to condom use karna chahiye , aisa..matlab mera aadmi agar kisi aurat ke saath sambandh karta hai to yeh condom use karna chahiye..R: To aapka kabhi mann nahin kiya ke condom istamaal karte hein? I: Nahin, kyonki mujhe poora yakeen hai unpe ke woh kisi aur ke paas nahin jaate , mere siwa, mere paas hi rehte hein R: If I tell you that a wife and husband use condom, how do u feel about it? I :Ganda lagta hai yeh baat R :Isme ganda kya lagta hai ? I: Yahi ke apni aurat ko karne mein condom kya lagaana , dossri aurat ke saath karna hai to laga sakta hai woh, apni aurat ke saath yeh sab kyon.. accha nahin lagta hai isliye"

"R: What did you hear about it on TV?

I: this that when men have relations with other women, then condoms should be used, for example if my man has a relation with another woman then we should use a condom.

131

R: So you never felt like using a condom?

I: No because I have full faith in him that he does not go to anyone else, other than me, he stays with me only.

R: If I tell you that a wife and husband use condom, how do u feel about it?

I: Hearing this feels bad.

R: What is bad in this?

I: This only that when one has to have sex with one's own wife, why should he use a condom, when he has sex with another woman then he can use it, but why with one's own wife. That's why it feels bad hearing this.

Interestingly, women in the study group whose husbands used condom felt easy and free to discuss with their husbands discontinuance of condom and choosing some other mode of contraception in case they (women) did not like condoms.

- **Trust issue , Husband does not like it**

  "Because it feels like I mistrusted him..." ("Kyonki unpe shakk kiya jaise hota hai naa.."

In the interview quoted below, the interview reported that she and her husband did not know much about condom before they came to know about their HIV positive status; Acc. to her Trust was too big a factor to use condom , they claimed having no reason to use condom as they did know that either of the partners was infected;

"R: When you did not know that both of you are HIV+, before that did you ever speak about condoms?

I: No, we never used it before because we never knew about it; we never knew something like this would happen to us. I did not even know that there was some problem with him or that I had some problem. We trusted each other and did everything, got married, got settled down, but now we don't know because of whom, the other partner got infected, that we do not know."(an HIV+ve woman)

4.3.2.4 Reasons given by married women for not using condom

As seen already most women prefer that their husbands take initiative /decision whether to use condom or not. Most studies highlight barriers to condom use as attitudinal for men, and predominantly structural for women, however not many have asked the question what do women think of using condom. While this study would also discuss these socio-cultural barriers, so intricately linked to women's sexual health and well-being, in the following section we would begin with some more reasons given by women themselves for not using condom. While these reasons are certainly not unknown, one question that has not been asked is as to why Indian women do not /do not want to use condom.

In an open ended semi structured questionnaire, women not using condom were asked to give reasons for not using condom. The main points that came out were validated through another close ended survey (administered to 100 women participants).

The following reasons were brought to light by the interviewees:

A: Condom is only for those people who go out /promiscuous

B: Condom is only for those people who are infected with STD s or HIV etc.

C: Husband does not like to use condom

D: Do not know about condom

E: Condom disgusts me

Table 4.9: Reasons given by the married women for not wanting to use condoms.

A:Condom is only for those people who go out /promiscuous	B:Condom is only for those people who are infected with STDs or HIV etc.	C: Husband does not like to use condom	D: Do not know about condom	E:Condom disgusts me
41%	24%	24%	10%	1%

Two main reasons that have contributed to negative image of condom, and consequently its low usage are:

- People who use condoms are those with multiple partners and those who visit sex workers.

- Condom is associated with treatment of sexually transmitted diseases.

In this survey it was revealed that majority of women associate condom with promiscuity (42 percent) and infection (24 percent). They perceive that condom is meant for those who are promiscuous and /or those who are already infected two things no woman would like to associate herself or her husband with, irrespective of the reality. These were two of the main reasons for women not using or wanting to ask their husbands to use condom.

> *"If husband is wrong then you can say use a condom, HIV/AIDS..."*

> *"We have all the information and knowledge, but if we don't go outside why should we use the condom, this has been made to save from diseases. We don't use it because we don't go outside, that's why we don't use condoms, and it's just this thing, no other matter."* (A woman interviewee's husband)

Negative attitudes towards condom use with wives is known to be one of the main reasons for men not wanting to use condom and their getting angry and /or violent when being asked by their wives to use it[53], not to mention that this also brings up the question of trust for partner. The **"Trust factor"** was found to be strongly linked to the fact that most women did not want to discuss using condom with their husbands– 89 percent of women believe that if they asked their partners to use condom, their husbands would feel that they are not trusted by their wives, while 82 percent of women believe that their husbands would think that they themselves are having sex outside.

> *"He will feel that either his wife is with someone else, that's why she says to use a condom, or else, the man if he says to use the*

---

[53] Table 4.5 - Percentage distribution of women who feel that their husbands would get angry/violent if they asked them to use condom.

condom, the wife will feel that the man is with some other woman.
That's why."

4.4 Communicating to Married women about Marital Violence, HIV / AIDS and Condom Use - Results and Findings

4.4.1 Knowledge about legal support

The Protection of Women from Domestic Violence Act 2005 was brought into force by the Indian government from October 26, 2006. This is a landmark law for the Indian women, as for the first time marital rape was recognized and prohibited by law. This law guarantees more protection of rights to the victims of domestic violence against any kind of physical, emotional, financial abuse from their partners. Prior to this law, Domestic violence was recognized as a criminal offence in India in 1983, under section 498-A of the Indian Penal Code. This section dealt with any form of cruelty by a husband or his family towards a married woman. However, at the time India did not have a law on marital rape. This meant that even if a woman's husband has sexual intercourse with her without her consent, he could not be prosecuted for rape.

Women were asked if they knew of the Domestic Violence (DV) Act 2005. Keeping in consideration that many women may not know of the law by its name, they were asked in simple language, if they had heard or knew of any such law which says that a husband cannot beat his wife, force his wife to sex etc., if he does so, he could be prosecuted or jailed.

Majority of women interviewed had not heard of any such law and did not know that a husband could be punished by law if he rapes his wife. Some of them said that a husband could be punished if he murders or beats his wife to death.

> *No, if there is a forceful relationship between the husband and wife then the law cannot give a punishment for it. If a stranger does it, then the law can punish him for that.*

> *"No can it be like that? He cannot go to jail.*

> *R: Why can't he go to jail?*

> *I: Only if he has killed the wife, has murdered the wife will he be in prison."*

> *"He should not do like this. The policeman will hit him, what's the use. She has to live off his earnings; she has to depend on him. So why do such a thing?*

> *R: What if the woman is not dependent on the husband financially?*

> *I: When that woman is with another man, then she does something like this to her husband. - Complains against him to the police."*

Most of the women interviewed had no knowledge of this new law (which was passed almost two years before this survey was done); neither did they know of any helplines. The interviewees were asked if they knew of any helpline, should they want to seek help in case of violence for themselves or for someone they know. None of them could give any helpline numbers other than the police emergency number 100, so they were told of two numbers -103[54] and 1298[55] , and were then asked if they had heard of both or any of the two numbers. None of the women had any knowledge of any of these two numbers.

---

[54] 103 helpline was launched on 28th February 2008 by the Mumbai Police, in collaboration with the Campaign against Violence against Women and Girls (VAW Campaign). Since 2010, the State home department made this helpline is operational all over Maharahtra.

For more information see, "Helpline 103 will now be for all women in Maharashtra."; "Soon, you can call 103 for help from any place in state".

[55] On January 28th, 2008, after assuming the post of the Sheriff of Mumbai, Dr. Indu Sahani launched the '1298' Women's Helpline in association with '1298 Ambulance Service' and 75 Women NGO's to help women against sexual harassment and violence.

For more information see, "1298 Women's Helpline."

4.4.2 Listening about condom/HIV/AIDS, is it enough?

4.4.2.1 Hearing about HIV/AIDS is not equal to using condoms

Lack of knowledge is one of the significant, though not the only factors that cuts and inhibits women's decision making power to use condom (cf: Reasons given by married women for not using condom).

Women interviewees who had heard about HIV/AIDS and condoms, admitted not having given a thought about using them, for reasons ranging from " incomplete or no knowledge at all about condoms,

> *No, have heard it on TV sometime, have heard the name but don't know what it is:*
>
> *R: You don't know what it is?*
>
> *I: No, but I have heard of it.*

lack of time and space to discuss it with husband,

> *I. They tell about the disease, like this and that, they say - One can get infected, should use a condom. That's what you said just now, that's only the sensible thing to do.*
>
> *R: So do you really believe that this is the sensible thing to do?*
>
> *I: He (her husband) says that it's the sensible thing to do.*

R: So you agree, so what is it that you don't find good? What is it that for others it may be a sensible thing to do, but not for you.

I: no, I did not even think like this ever.

R: Why did you not think?

I: Never thought like this, no.

R: But why did you not think like this?

I: I don't know why, my husband did not think of it, we did not think, no one thought of it, because in our house, we only have a very small room, that's why we never get the time, because the children are at home, my in-laws stay at home, when they go out then we get a chance to meet.

To considering HIV and condom to be vile topic, meant only for people who "do something wrong". Majority of women ignored listening to the information given to them or following it mostly because they admitted being unable to relate themselves with the information given to them. Risk perception among almost all of them was not just low but virtually nonexistent. Condom is viewed by most as prevention of infection than contraception (cf. why condom not as popular is a contraceptive?).

"...Wife should tell husband that I do not want a child, so use condom.... And also for HIV/AIDS.. so if wife explains

142

her husband , he will definitely listen and understand. So did you ever tell your husband to use condom? I: No R: Why not? I: Nothing happened ("kucch hua hi nahin to")(giggles) If husband would do something wrong then I can tell him to use condom...HIV/AIDS(agar pati galat hoga to main bol sakti hai naa ke condom use karo, HIV/AIDS..) .

Women who may have heard about HIV/AIDS and or condoms may not necessarily have much about either of the two. Most women in this survey admitted not caring to listen to the information given to them on this topic as they did not believe it concerned them in any way. As one HIV +ve interviewee admitted;

> *"Used to hear about HIV/AIDS on the television but would simply ignore It thinking who cares, it may be some disease ("hogi koi bimaari......".) like any other....*

4.4.2.2 Influence of television on women's knowledge and motivation to use condoms

In this study, women (N=100) were asked in a close–ended survey to identify the source from where they had heard about HIV/AIDS and then they were asked open-ended questions about their opinions regarding the information given to them. 37 percent of women who had heard about HIV/AIDS reported television as their principal source of information. This percentage is less than the NHFS-3 data as per which Television is by far the most common source of information on AIDS, reported by 80 percent of women who have

143

heard of AIDS, which also includes women from a higher wealth index as compared to the study group.

The interviewees who said that they had heard about HIV/AIDS on television were later asked their opinion about the quality of information they received on television. While some of the women interviewed found the televised information too brief, some even mentioned that they had heard about HIV/AIDS but did not know how to prevent it;

> *R: 1st time you heard of it on TV?*
>
> *I: Yes I saw it on TV*
>
> *R: Did you feel that the information you are getting from TV was it enough?*
>
> *I: No, because on TV they don't tell everything, even if they told everything I would not have understood it all*
>
>
> *R: Please tell me have you heard of HIV/AIDS?*
>
> *I: I don't know much*
>
> *R: You don't know much but have you heard of it? Where have you heard of it?*
>
> *I: It comes on TV.*

Those who had heard about condoms claimed not having much knowledge about its advantages or how to use it;

R: You don't use it but do you know of condoms? Have you heard of condoms from somewhere?

I: If I have not used it then how will I come to know of it?

R: But have you heard of it?

I: yes, now when it comes on TV then I have seen it

R: What are the benefits of condoms? (R is about to tell I about its uses but is interrupted by I)

I: I don't know all that

R: Continues to tell uses of condom, other than contraceptive, ... are there any other benefits?

I: I don't know

(R: tells about condom as preventive for infection)

I: I have understood, I did not know all that.

I: I did not understand what you mean by condom?

R: explains about condom, .. have you ever used it?

I: no, no

R: Have you ever talked about it?

I: no, I don't even know about it

R: You have never spoken about it? Have you ever heard of it?

I: Once I heard of it on TV, many days back.

others admitted being indifferent to the information given to them saying that it was not their problem ,"did not know and did not care to know" about HIV/AIDS.

> *"Came to know from TV, but got more information when my second child died. Use to watch and listen but just like it must be some disease, but when I came to know of my HIV+ status, then I understood more. If I knew about it before I would have been able to save myself. My husband may have been infected but I could have saved myself. If I knew of it before it would have been very good. One should listen about it, now they tell everything openly it is a good thing. First I used to get scared, now I don't even feel scared.*

I: TV ke upar... suna hoga par hum log ko aisa faltoo...

I: On TV, I may have heard but we people don't want to listen to such useless things...

4.4.3 How would married women want to receive information regarding intimate topics relative to sexual reproductive health?

In this study women interviewees were asked;

- Who do they feel free to discuss intimate issues with regarding sexual reproductive health, especially if they have sex related issues /problems?

- How they would like to get information about private intimate stuff, like condom usage, personal body, etc. TV, radio or would she prefer that someone like me or a doctor comes to their house to explain...?

Table 4.10: If they had sex related issues, who would they/should they discuss it with?

Person	%
Husband	13
Doctor	69
Mother	3
Sister	0
Friend	15
	100

Table 4.11: How would they like to get information about private intimate stuff , like condom usage, personal body , etc.

Medium	%
Doctor	48
Hospital	15
TV	33
Radio	4
	100

The above two questions were asked to understand who they were comfortable with discussing these topics. Majority of women feel free to discuss sex related health issues with a doctor, followed by friends and spouse, very few would discuss this with their immediate female relatives such as mother or sister etc. (none of them felt free to discuss it with male relatives other than their own husbands). Not only do they feel free to discuss sexual health issues with doctors, most of them prefer to seek relative information from an expert such as doctor, preferably and understandably a female doctor rather than from TV or radio.

"The thing with posters is that not a lot is written in them, on TV also they don't say a lot. Doctors can explain better about such things."

"I don't see TV so much, if a doctor will tell, he will do it with good intentions so I will feel better."

"TV radio se zyada har mohalle mein camps lage , ghar ghar mein jaake bataayein to uska zyada faayda hoga"

"It is better than TV and radio that in every area there are camps, that they go to every house and tell, that will be more beneficial."

The second question also accesses their freedom of movement, while majority prefer to get information from a doctor, as someone they can trust , most of them wanted that a doctor visits them home, only 17 percent responded that they can go to a hospital to get the required information, if they are called .

4.4.4 How would married women prefer marital domestic violence to be addressed as a social issue through Audio-visual medium, for instance television?

During the in-depth interviews, when one of the respondents was asked with what medium she would like to know more about the topic of Marital Domestic Violence, she responded that she would like to receive this information in the form of a Talk show. This added a new medium to the researcher's list of Films and Serials. 39 women out of 75 were asked this question with the medium of Talkshow included in it.

Table 4.12 presents the results from the in-depth interviews regarding women interviewees' opinions/preferences as to medium through which the issue of marital DV may be addressed.

This interview talk show (it's a good way), we can bring forth our problems and issues and they can offer use guidance and advice, and we can thus get information we need.

Like they sit face to face on TV, If such issues and problems are brought up on TV, lots of people are interested to watch, and they get informed at the same time...... ...what's there in a film or movie, people watch, enjoy, go home and forget all about the real issue.....in a way like this talk show, everyone can be informed what the issue if all about.........!

No one takes movies seriously, that it's just a movie, in most cases, like you (indicating researcher) are talking, women would listen and believe that it is an important issue that is being talked about that it is important to listen to it...... no one takes movies or serials very seriously as they believe that such things don't happen in real life...

Table 4.12: In what mediums would they like the issue of Marital Domestic Violence to be addressed in the audio-visual media e.g. on Television (data from In-depth Interviews)

Medium	No.	%
Film	1	3
Talkshow	32	82
Serials	6	15
	39	100

Later on the researcher validated once again this question with the 100 survey participants. The results from these presented below in table 4.13.

Table 4.13: In what mediums would they like the issue of Marital Domestic Violence to be addressed in the audio-visual media e.g. on Television (data from Survey)

Medium	%
Film	46
Talkshow	22
Both Talkshows and Films	4
Serials	26
Unsure / Don't know	2
	100

4.5 Conclusion

This chapter presented the findings in regards to the married women's perceptions and attitudes in regards to Domestic Marital Violence - both physical and sexual and condoms. It presents this using rich narrative from the in-depth interviews and using the women's own words. As seen from these findings, they have a tolerant attitude towards marital violence from reasons ranging from financial dependency to shame and for the sake of the little children. On the other hand, it was observed that condom acceptability was low among the married women, due to reasons such as unfelt need - want to have children, sterilizations to negative associations with condoms. Finally in the third section, it was seen that the knowledge of the women about the Domestic Violence Act as well as other legal and other support available was found to be sparse and almost negligible. It was also seen that even if they had heard of condoms they did not find the information received very relevant and could not relate to it. These findings are further discussed and interpreted in the next chapter.

5. Discussion

5.1 Introduction

In this chapter, I discuss the findings from the research (presented in Chapter 4) and interpret their meaning using the lens of the existing literature and prior studies, and present in more detail some of the findings that are especially interesting or surprising.

5.2 Discussion: Marital violence

The findings on marital violence in the previous chapter highlight some of the attitudes and beliefs of women on spousal violence, including sexual abuse. To the researcher's knowledge, this is the first qualitative study to take into account married Indian women's beliefs regarding marital rape and forced unsafe sex and how they *believe* a wife must cope with forced sex, including forced unsafe sex. In this study, it was seen that most women agreed that a wife should tolerate being physically and/or sexually abused by her husband. The most common reasons given for tolerating physical abuse were for the sake of the family, especially children, as well as for the wife's own sake; it is worth tolerating as long as the husband is providing well for them and their children. Some of them further

153

justified wife beating if it was not too often, not too much and if the reason for the beating was justified, i.e. if the wife has transgressed in some manner, e.g., lying to her husband, going somewhere without telling him, etc. In contrast to tolerating physical abuse for a variety of the above-mentioned reasons, a majority of women believed that wives should tolerate sexual abuse by their husbands. The results of this current study indicate that majority of women believed that violence (physical/sexual) should be tolerated, regardless of the "threshold". Our findings thus partially corroborate a qualitative study (Vivian F. Go et al. 2003)[56] conducted in a similar research setting in south India which highlighted three main dimensions of the social acceptability of violence: intensity, justification and frequency. While only a small percentage of married women (21 percent) in my study expressed the opinion that physical violence should be tolerated within a certain threshold. 55 percent believed that women should tolerate violence, irrespective of the conditions, for the sake of family and children. The percentage of

[56] The objective of this study was to examine the pathways by which gender norms may influence marital violence in low-income communities of Chennai, India and understand the patterns and trigger factors for violence within a domestic setting.

[57] One of the reasons could be that program managers mostly rely more on quantitative rather than qualitative data to put an issue on priority agenda. Unfortunately, there have been no large scale population surveys quantitatively demonstrating a causal link between domestic, sexual violence and a married woman victim's increased vulnerability to HIV/AIDS. Hence, the causal link between sexual violence and HIV/AIDS remains to date unaddressed by policy makers in India.

It has been seen however that, *"the culturally endowed "privacy" and"secrecy" surrounding sex renders sexual violence against women an almost unspeakable matter, especially within the family context"* (Mo Yee Lee and Phyllis. "Perception of Sexual Violence against Women in Asian American Communities." 2001.

married women who did not accept sexual violence outside this threshold was even smaller (5 percent). Reasons for tolerating sexual abuse ranged from "husband has complete rights over his wife", "sake of child" to "honor of family and self". This latter reason is consistent with other studies showing that women victims, especially those brought up in traditional societies, endure or remain silent to keep their family honor intact (Dasgupta 2000; Yee Lee & Phyllis F. M., 2001). [57] Also, a multicountry study by the WHO showed that even if women left their husbands after an incident of abuse, those who returned gave reasons such as they could not leave their children, or "for the sake of the family". Other reasons were that the woman loved her partner, that he had asked her to come back, that she had forgiven him or thought he would change, or because the family had said she should return. Women who never left gave similar reasons as well as indicated that they did not know where to go (Garcia-Moreno et al. 2005).

This study expands on the existing literature by providing rich qualitative data in the participant interviewees' own words about their opinions; on tolerating physical and sexual violence within the marital sphere, and more importantly, their views on marital rape.

In regard to marital rape, although most women admitted that if the husband forces his wife against her will it is forced sex, they did not acknowledge it as rape. One of the main reasons given for this was that rape is something committed by a stranger not by one's own husband, regardless of the wife's concurrence, and also that a husband has complete rights over his wife. Their response to cope with forced unsafe sex was not different from what is expected of "good wives". The majority believed that a wife should tolerate sexual violence by the husband silently[58], as that is what a "good wife" should do, and it is the only way to keep their honor intact within and outside the family.

These findings are supported by the NHFS-3 data, which showed that only one in four women have ever sought help to end the violence they have experienced. Moreover, two out of three women who have experienced violence also never it with anyone. A large majority of women who have experienced only sexual violence have never told anyone about the violence (85 percent), and only 8 percent have ever sought help. In a study done to investigate the causes and consequences of marital rape, Frieze (1983) was told by many of the married woman interviewees that they had been pressured to have sex but would not define their experiences as "rape," even though their descriptions of the incidents met all the standard legal criteria for rape. While studying domestic violence in the South Asian community in the United States, Dasgupta stated that "South Asian cultural socialization may also render women perplexed about the appropriateness of their realities. For example, South Asian victims tend to recognize physical abuse quite readily and yet, are most reluctant to acknowledge sexual coercion and/or abuse". He further points out that his 15 years of work with battered South Asian women shows that the majority are convinced that marriage denies

---

[58] High and silent tolerance rate for spousal, physical and or sexual abuse may be the reason for fewer women admitting to spousal violence in public and consequently for the lower rate of spousal violence recorded in the national data.(IIPS and Macro International. NHFS-3,2007)

them the right to have any sexual control. Moreover, most women believe that marital vows confer upon husbands the right to have unquestioned sexual access to their wives' bodies. To many women, "marital rape" is an alien concept. He supports his argument by citing Mazumdar (1998), who also asserts that this sentiment is a traditional South Asian cultural phenomenon.[59]

In this study, 37 percent and 12 percent of the women participants reported physical and sexual marital violence respectively. These results are in accord with the NHFS data. This research expands on previous data by showing that while 12 percent of participants reported sexual violence by their husbands, 69 percent reported submitting to unwanted sex with their husbands mostly out of fear, i.e. in order not to annoy the husband, and also as an obligation of a "good wife". Such observations suggest that the reason that few women report or acknowledge marital rape may lie in avoidance of a possible escalation into violence.

The results of this study suggest that in cases of forced unwanted sex, the majority of women prefer to remain silent, instead of seeking help (from family or police). Given the socio-cultural environment, the significance of reporting physical and/or sexual abuse has so far been greatly underestimated in India, especially by married women and their families, and sometimes even by the authorities such as the police. As most women choose to or are made to stay at home instead of seeking external help, they are deprived of

---

[59] Only when physical violence, sexual perversity, and/or sexual torture compound sexual coercion do women perceive their experiences as abusive (Abraham, 1999- cited in Dasgupta SD 2000)."

essential information to protect themselves. A small community-based study in Pune, India, showed that women reporting such abuse were more than twice as likely to have adequate HIV/AIDS knowledge compared with women reporting no such abuse (Shrotri et al 2003). Societal attitudes as well as (sometimes) attitudes of the family of the victims may result in victims being blamed and a lack of support for the victims of marital violence (Garcia and Juan Herrero 2006; George 1998). This may lead the victims of marital violence to be silent sufferers of their abuse. According to Garcia, by reducing social tolerance and inhibition and by increasing identification and reporting of domestic violence against women, steps may be taken to remedy the situation of domestic violence (Garcia 2004).

Women's responses to the topic of forced unsafe sex were identical to those for forced sex. The majority indicated that a wife should tolerate forced unsafe sex silently. It should be noted that unsafe sex for married women in general is no different from unwanted sex because they do not perceive a need for a condom (cf. why women do not use condoms). One of the main reasons for this may be their low self-risk perception, which has also been noted among wives of men practicing high-risk behavior (Panda et al. 2005). Interestingly, however, when asked about their reaction to unsafe sex, they believed that a woman has the right to refuse and protect herself, *if* her husband is infected or has multiple sexual relations, and could,if need be, even escalate the issue by going to elders . This finding is consistent with the NHFS data, which shows that 78-79 percent of women agree that a wife has the right to refuse her husband sex if he has an STD. Unfortunately, as many as 22 percent of married Indian women deny themselves their sexual rights in dire situations. Compared to women, the majority of adult men in India (89 percent) say that a woman can refuse to have sex or ask her husband to use a condom if she knows that he has an STI. Men's agreement with the right of women to negotiate safe sex, either by refusing sex or by asking the man to use a condom, indicates an extremely conducive environment for ensuring safe sexual practices among women and men (IIPS and Macro International -NHFS-3 2007). Women in this study nevertheless raised the concern that most women would not know of their husband's HIV/AIDS status or his clandestine relations, and without this knowledge, a wife may not be in a position to refuse unprotected sex. Previous studies show that women who knew about their husband's HIV positive status were significantly more likely to always use condoms than those who did not think their husband was HIV positive or did not know the husband's status (Mehta et al. 2006); however, condom use was not consistent/universal (Solomon et al. 2010). The reasons could range from being subject to social norms to (fear of) sexual coercion.

Fear of violence is another key factor known to play a key role in increasing women's reluctance to use condoms and limiting their capacity for condom negotiation. As noted by Go et al. (2003), *"given the choice between the immediate and tangible threat of violence versus the relatively hypothetical specter of HIV, women often resign themselves to a husband's sexual indiscretions and sexual demands"*.

Another major point of consideration also discussed above is that the fear of violence embedded in women's minds influences them to opt for non consensual unsafe sex. The results from this study suggest that the fear of a husband's anger and /or violence represents one of the reasons for women not wanting to negotiate safe sex. This finding corroborates other studies underscoring that fear of domestic violence among women is one of the major barriers to establishing and maintaining control over their own sexuality and their husbands' sexual activity outside of marriage (Njovana and Watts 1996; Go et al. 2003; Bhattacharya 2004). Consequently, wives are exposed to unsafe marital sex as fear of domestic violence limits their ability to refuse sex to husband and negotiate safe sex within marital setting (Bujra J. 2000; Verma and Collumbien 2003; Ali, Cleland, and Shah 2004; Varma et al. 2010; Swan and O'Connell 2011), thereby increasing their risk of being infected with a sexually transmitted disease, including HIV (Wingood and DiClemente 1997). Of the 75 participants (from Mumbai and Delhi), very few women (19) reported condom use with their husbands, and of those 19, 11 women reported being physically forced to have sex without condoms even in cases where condom usage was preferred, indicating a lack of autonomy in safe sex negotiation. Furthermore, a majority of women (75 percent) reported not using condoms during sex with their husbands. Interestingly, most of them did not show any particular interest or need to use them. This led the researcher to further explore the reasons for low condom use and low acceptability among the women interviewees.

To summarize, this study suggests three important findings: Firstly, most women agree that a wife *should tolerate* spousal abuse, physical or sexual, by her husband; secondly, they feel that forced sex by the husband cannot be acknowledged as rape; and thirdly, the majority believe that a women should *silently tolerate unwanted sex, including forced unsafe sex.* The only exception noted was in cases where the wife has knowledge about her husband's infection or his high-risk behavior; in such situations, the wife has the right of refusal.

Previous research underlines that that wife-beating is deeply entrenched in India and that normative attitudes condone and justify wife-beating, making it acceptable to such a degree that few women choose to escape an abusive marriage (Jeejebhoy 1998; Koenig et al. 2006). This underscores a strong and urgent need for strategies to combat violence. There is an even more pressing reason to integrate domestic violence into HIV prevention interventions. It is important to acknowledge that domestic violence does not place all women at risk of HIV/AIDS; nevertheless, evidence clearly indicates an increased risk for HIV infection among women experiencing sexual violence from their husbands (Silverman et al. 2008; Ghosh et al. 2011) and that partners perpetrating violence are more likely than other men to engage in HIV risk behaviors (Silverman et al. 2008). For instance, findings from a cross–sectional Indian study by Solomon et al (2011) on the spouses of intravenous drug users (IDUs) revealed that the risk of HIV among their wives was tenfold compared to the general population and was compounded by factors such as high levels of intimate partner violence (IPV) , including forced sex. With respect to various types of violence, 85.5% of the women indicated experiencing sexual violence (forced to have sex against their will). The same study underlines two very significant points: Firstly, that women were generally powerless in this situation as the majority of these women were unaware of their husband's drug abuse before marriage. When they ultimately discovered his drug history, it was "too late" for them to change their situation as divorce is not perceived as a common option within Indian society, particularly in lower socio economic communities. According to Solomon et al., *"This situation appears to produce a volatile environment; one in which resources are strained and stability is thereby affected, leading to high levels of violence and disease transmission."* (Solomon et al. 2011).

Strategies to combat violence are urgently needed, and these must address not only the immediate needs of battered women but must also attack the root cause of violence - women's "powerlessness" (Jeejebhoy 1998). As aptly noted by Jeejebhoy, *the need to reverse social attitudes and beliefs that legitimize male violence and the notion of male superiority at the family level among women, their husbands, family elders, and society at large* (Jeejebhoy 1998).

5.3 Discussion: Condom Use, Condom Acceptability
& Contraception Choices

Studies show that women who perceive the control of husbands over their wives as justified, can be considered less empowered than women who think otherwise (Correa and Petchesky, 1994; Sen and Batliwala, 2000; United Nations, 1995a; 1995b. - cited in Kishore and Gupta 2009).This may also hold true for women who do not perceive themselves as a joint agency in sexual decision making. Women who believe that husbands should have more say in the matter are more likely to have little decision-making power in real life regarding such issues (cf. Married women` s expectations of her sexual rights in marriage, p 85).

This preference that husbands be the decision makers, is however limited only to the extent that the health and well being of the women are not being compromised. The data from this study also yielded similar results indicating that a majority (78 percent) of women would refuse unprotected / unsafe sex if their husbands were infected with an STD and/or HIV/AIDS. The data from the current research is in line with a national health family survey which suggests that the majority of women in India do reject norms that say that "a wife should not refuse her husband sex", especially under circumstances such as if husband has an STD or more so if he has sex with another woman. As per NHFS data, 77 percent of women agree that a woman is justified in refusing sex to her husband when

163

she knows that he has a sexually transmitted disease (STD) (Kishore and Gupta 2009).

Making condoms a choice contraceptive offers the possibility of responding to two issues at the same time. Firstly, it will help prevent HIV infection among one of the most vulnerable populations, young married women in their reproductive prime, and also their unborn babies. Secondly, it helps the government achieve its important goal of slowing down the fertility rate. However, discontinuation of contraceptive methods has always been a major concern for family planning managers. As expected, it was seen in this study that temporary contraceptive use, including condom use, was extremely low among the study sample group. This study shows two principal reasons for not using contraceptives. Firstly, contraception is rejected in favor of reproduction, a finding which is supported by NHFS-3, which shows that the most frequently mentioned reason for discontinuing a method is to become pregnant, followed by concerns about side effects or health concerns. For condoms, the most frequently cited reason for discontinuation is the desire to become pregnant (IIPS and Macro International NHFS-3 2007). The age-group of 15-49 accounts for the highest number of HIV-infected cases in India. As this is the reproductive age group, there is a significant risk becoming infected and then passing on the disease to their children.

The second and more interesting reason for not using a condom is that most of the women had already opted for female sterilization or were planning to do so in near future, as soon as their family was complete. This finding is also consistent with NHFS-3 data, which shows that female sterilization is the most widely used method (37.3 percent) among all other modes of contraception. Studies conducted in the past show that most couples who had adopted sterilization had not used any other family planning method in their reproductive life (ORG, 1990; Khan and Patel, 1996 - cited in Khan and Patel 1997). This means that these women did not be use condom to prevent pregnancy in their sexual relations, marital or non-marital. If HIV infection is a potential threat to couples who have already opted for sterilization, it is important that they use condoms as a preventive measure against HIV infection. This will be a major task for the family planning or HIV control program in India[60].

However, despite the target-free approach[61] adopted by the Indian government, sterilization is the mainstay of the Indian family

---

[60] Discussing women's reproductive health security and HIV/AIDS in India, Pallikadavath and Stones strongly stress that "the crucial issue that needs to be addressed is the shift required in the family planning program of India. The family planning program in India has been predominantly a sterilization program, although it does not officially favor any particular method explicitly. They strongly underline the need for a shift from the implicit emphasis on the sterilization program if condom use is to be truly popularized/ increased as a part of the family planning program. According to them, this needs to happen at all levels, from top management to the grass roots level workers at the sub primary health centre (sub-PHC) level of the public health system in India. On a positive note, under the current contraceptive target-free system, which became operational in 1997, it may be easier to make such a shift in emphasis to condom use from sterilization in the family planning program. They strengthen their argument and make it more appropriate by focusing on the fact that about nine-tenths of HIV positive individuals worldwide do not know they are infected: the only safe options are sex without penetration or sexual intercourse protected by condom use [UNAIDS 2000b:11]. In India, the majority of the HIV-infected population would also not know their HIV status. Thus, the sooner the Indian family planning program re-focuses on condom promotion, the better it would be for HIV prevention and control". (Pallikadavath and Stones. "Women's reproductive health security and HIV/AIDS in India." 2003).

planning program. In order to achieve its millennium development goals, the Indian government has decided to push the incentive-based family planning measure, mainly sterilisation. Recently, the National Population Stabilisation Fund[62] launched schemes such as PRERNA, "a responsible parenthood strategy" (as per the fund). One of the mandatory conditions to qualify for the incentive is a 36-month gap between the first and second child and the sterilization of one parent after the second child is born (Reward of Rs.7000/ if it is a girl child & Rs 5000/ if it is a boy). Preference is given to younger couples (age of wife not exceeding 30 years). Another scheme launched by the fund is "Santushti". Under the "Santushti" strategy private gynecologists and NSV surgeons are encouraged to perform 100 tubectomy / vasectomy operations in the public-private partnership mode[63].

Such lucrative schemes not only undermine the status of women in a patriarchal society such as India's, but they also deny women the right of informed choices by health professionals or merely pushed by their husbands to opt for sterilization. Such a strong social marketing of sterilization in the name of family planning is a big

[61] In 2000, the National Population Policy advocated a holistic, multisectoral approach to population stabilization, with no targets for specific contraceptive methods except for achieving a national average total fertility rate (TFR) of 2.1 by the year 2010. This resulted in a shift in implementation from centrally fixed targets to target-free dispensation through a decentralized, participatory approach.

[62] Also known as Jansankhya Stiratha Kosh (JSK)

[63] JSK offers a Rs. 15,000/- start- up advance and Rs. 500/- per case extra if 30 or more operations are conducted in a day in accredited hospitals or nursing homes. These modifications are promoted by JSK to encourage private sector involvement in offering services.

obstacle to success of condom promotion and HIV prevention programs. It should be noted that among women of other age groups, HIV prevalence is higher among those aged 30-39 years. Also interestingly, sterilization is a highly adopted method among this same age group (47.2 – 53 percent). Encouraging couples to opt for sterilization would mean lower use of condoms and only time will tell if this could translate into higher HIV infections within the younger age groups.

Table 5.1: Age wise data of HIV infected people and Use of female sterilisation as mode of contraception

Age (years)	HIV prevalence among women (percentage %)	Use of female sterilisation as mode of contraception (percentage %)
20-24	0.23	13.4
25-29	0.38	33.4
30-34	0.83	47.2
35-39	0.34	53.1

Source: India: DHS, 2005-06 (Ch 05- family planning; Ch- 12- HIV prevalence)

Another interesting finding from this study highlights a variety of reasons for the lack of popularity of condoms among married women. The reasons ranged from "do not feel the need to use condoms" to the issue of trust. Women who know about condoms but do not use them told the researcher that they did not feel the need to use condoms as they were either using some other mode of contraception or were sterilized. Even more interestingly, given the fact that they were already "protected" against pregnancy, interviewees indicated that condoms were unnecessary and were only used by those who seek to prevent infections like HIV/AIDS. None of the women regarded themselves as being at risk of infection[64]

168

and hence did not believe that they needed condoms. Some of the women also expressed personal disgust as a reason for not wanting to use condoms. Women participants gave a variety of reasons were given for finding condoms disgusting, such as the issue of disposal and inconvenience; personal bad experience (tearing of the condom during intercourse, which resulted in an unwanted pregnancy). This finding is consistent with previous studies which found that male participants also found condoms "dirty, repulsive and of poor quality" (Khan and Patel 1997; Sharma et al. 1997; Bentley et al. 1998; Balaiah 1999). Another reason for women developing a dislike for condoms is their negative association with promiscuity. While women may not be able to control decision making regarding condom use, this study shows that they may be able to influence the non-use of condoms. A few of the participants reported that their husbands stopped using condoms with them once they (women participants) expressed disgust and wished to discontinue the use of condoms. This finding is particularly interesting in the sense that the women's negative association of condoms with promiscuity may discourage even willing husbands from using condoms with their wives. Studies from other parts of the world have shown that men often fear that proposing to use a condom in steady relationship, including with their wives, may result in a suspicion of an extramarital affair (Ackermann and Klerk 2002; Bauni & Jarabi 2003). In this study, it was also seen that the trust factor was strongly associated with women not wanting to discuss condom use

[64] Low risk perception among women is one of the factors observed by studies documenting risk factors for HIV infection among monogamous married women. For more information on this point, see Newmann et al. 2000; Chatterjee and Hosain 2006; Silverman et al. 2008,etc.

with their husbands. A study from southern India shows that among other barriers (such as inconvenience, or the lack of the condom's appeal), the stigma associated with condom negotiation severely limits the prospect of condom use, especially by wives (Sri Krishnan et al. 2007).

Many studies have observed that for most married men and women, condoms are associated with outside partners and hence should be used only for casual sex and with prostitutes (Changanti et al. 1994- cited in Bauni and Jarabi 2003; Bujra 2000). The study by Bauni also strongly indicates that being associated with unfaithfulness, condoms are not acceptable in most stable sexual relationships, including marriage. Bauni and Jarabi (2003) observe that being associated with infidelity, possession or use of condoms within marriage or in a steady relationship implies lack of trust of partner hence a potential cause for a breakup. It is the fear of the resultant feelings and subsequent consequences that constitutes the major obstacle to condom use to prevent STIs including HIV in stable sexual relationships. Despite the male dominance in making decisions over a wide range of family issues, including sex, husbands also fear asking their wives to use condoms (since they do not want to create suspicion that they have affairs outside of marriage). Being associated with infidelity, condoms have become symbols of unfaithfulness and can cause mistrust in relationships (Bujra 2000) -" *Trust and risk counter point each other....Trust enhances the danger of infection But Risk also equalizes it , putting both men and women into situation where the Other could kill* (Bujra 2000, p 78) . Hence they challenge the very basis of human relationships — trust and willingness to put one's life into another's hands' (Bond and Dover, 1997; Bujra 2000).

This data is consistent with other studies showing that one of the main reasons that condoms remain so unpopular and fail to appeal to the masses is the stigma associated with their use (Gamson 1990; Lupton 1994; Steven W. Sinding 2005;Sarkar 2008). Many women and men feel shame about using them and frequently refuse to use condoms within marriage because of the association in many people's minds between condoms and illicit sex (Nicols 1990 – cited in Wingood and DiClemente 1998; Bond and Dover, 1997; Maharaj and Cleland, 2004; Sinding, 2005). Many people also tend to associate condoms with STDs and HIV/AIDS (Bledsoe 1991:8; Preston-Whyte 1993:9 (see bond and dover 1997); Maliki et al. 2006; Plummer at al .2006). This social stigma associated with condoms is one of the most significant barriers to acquiring, carrying, and using condoms (Roth, Krishnan, and Bunch 2001; Helweg-Larsen & Collins 1994, Sacco et al. 1993 - cited in Dahl et al. 2005).

According to Lupton (1994*), "First used as a prophylactic against sexually transmitted disease, and traditionally worn in encounters with prostitutes, the condom before the advent of AIDS had acquired a negative image as a symbol of furtive and socially unacceptable sexuality" (p. 304).*

Findings on married women's expectations in their sexual life (cf. table 4.7) show that a majority of women prefer their husband to take the initiative and make decisions regarding their sexual life,

171

including condom use. These findings indicate the need for more male involvement in sexual reproductive decision making. Given that a husband's attitude about contraception influences his wife's opinion and eventual adoption of a contraceptive method (Chandhick et al. 2003), men's attitudes toward contraception are bound to have a significant effect on the success or failure of family planning programs in the community (Balaiah et al. 1999; Saluja et al. 2011). Women need to have men as partners in reproductive health— partners who understand the risks they might be exposed to and strategies for their prevention.

Although HIV risk awareness is increasing, few men report condom use or appropriate changes in their behavior to minimize their risk (Mbizvo and Bassett 1996; Dhingra et al. 2010)). According to Mbizvo and Bassett (1996), the female bias in family planning (FP) programs ignores the fact that in this setting, men often control the use of contraceptives by their wives. The inclusion of men in FP and reproductive health decision making has been shown to be favorable to the increase in contraceptive usage (Balaiah et al 1999; Terefe and Larson 1993, Robey and Drennan 1998 – cited in Yadav and Singh 2010). Therefore, it may be important to motivate and educate not just women, but to actively involve both men and women as a couple in contraceptive decisions making (Chankapa, Pal, and Tsering 2010).

As already discussed above, despite the fact that men are as familiar with condoms as they are with female sterilization, the percentage of

172

use of female sterilization surpasses the use of condoms. This shows that merely increasing awareness has not and will not lead to the adoption of condom use. Previous studies underline the need to educate men on the importance of using condoms and motivate them to increase condom acceptability among men. This also includes countering negative perceptions about modern contraceptive methods, especially condoms (Bajwa et al. 2011), which should, in turn, make contraceptive decision making as well as condom negotiation easier for married women. Also, increasing male involvement in family planning will not detract from efforts to improve the status of women; rather, it may, in the long run, lead to enhanced communication within marriages and greater decision-making equality for women (Farosay 1989 - cited in Piotrow et al. 1992). Such a shift would potentially have the added benefit of preventing HIV infections (Ali, Cleland and Shah 2004).

Condom use has been promoted for over three decades in India but it remains the least popular and consequently least used method of contraception. It is important for structural barriers like gender inequality to be addressed; however, even if we bring about gender equality and women start enjoying equal sexual decision-making power, there will be no increase in demand for condoms by men or women if they continue to be negatively associated with promiscuity and STDs. From a marketing point of view, policy makers and condom promoters must break this negative association and create a fresh new positive image of condoms, if mass adoption of condoms is the goal.

"Despite the attempts of health promoters and condom manufacturers to make condoms respectable, they still seem to suffer from stigmatization. Continued lack of popularity of condoms, by demonstrating the deep cultural anxieties and negative meanings that still surround them. Until these are challenged, it is unlikely that the general population will adopt the use of condoms to protect against the spread of AIDS."(Lupton, 1994).

5.4 Discussion: Communicating to the Married women about Marital Violence, HIV/AIDS and Condom Use

One of the initial efforts to help empower women was the implementation of the DV Act 2005. The PWDVA was enacted with the objective of protecting women from all forms of domestic violence. In defining domestic violence, the Act went beyond mere physical forms of violence, to include mental, sexual and economic violence. In its written form, its distinctive feature is that it provides women with a civil remedy. It also prescribes strict penalties for the breach of protection orders. Moreover, the role of the protection officer (PO) as a primary link between the victim and the court is a significant step toward emboldening women to initiate legal action against perpetrators. However, the results from this study indicate that the women interviewed were not well informed about the Domestic Violence Act and its special provisions provided under this Act, nor did they know of the helplines which exist in this regard. This finding is in line with the third monitoring and evaluation report of the PWDVA 2005, prepared by the Lawyers Collective. The report clearly indicates that, the lack of awareness about the law and its provisions for the benefit of women victims of domestic violence is one of reasons that domestic violence remains under reported and the law underutilized.

Media representations gain influence because people's social construction of reality depends heavily on what they see, hear, and

175

read rather than what they experience (Bandura 2004).Television and radio are media of mass reach. Like films they can reach a vast audience and help to disseminate the idea of social change in an effective way. In the recent past, TV and radio started being used to address various social issues through the Entertainment-Education model and has been strongly advocated by communication strategists and not without reason. Entertainment-education (E-E) is the process of purposely designing and implementing a media message to both entertain and educate in order to increase audience members' knowledge about an educational issue, create favorable attitudes, shift social norms, and change overt behavior (Singhal & Rogers 1999). Most importantly, the entertainment component of such programs provides an opportunity for an instructional message to pay for itself and fulfill commercial and social interests (Brown, 1991; Piotrow, 1990; Singhal & Rogers, 1989b – cited in Singhal & Rogers 1999).

In this regard, women participants were asked to indicate their (audio-visual) media preference (films; serials; talk shows) for addressing a topic such as domestic violence. Of the 40 women who were asked the question, 32 (80 percent) said that they would prefer talk shows. Talk shows were perceived to be deeper in terms of discussing the topic as well as offering concrete solutions and approaches to deal with the topic. This allowed the women to explore the issue in greater depth and to think of practical measures which they could take. For example, respondents indicated that, Aap Ki Kachehri Kiran Ke Saath[65] ("Your court with Kiran"[66]), a

[65] "Courting trouble"

televised Indian reality-justice show about real-life situations, is a show which they watch regularly and which informs them and presents them with a better understanding of the citizens' rights and the workings of Indian legal system.

Of the three media, only talk shows can be informational, exposing audiences to issues and topics that they would not be normally exposed to, cost effective as important messages can be delivered to millions of households at the same time, and orient people positively in an entertaining way. Talk shows can also be therapeutic by providing the participants a platform to open up and, share their experiences; they can encourage others to do the same, and importantly, can be solution oriented by informing and educating audiences about existing solutions, as well as creating new innovative solutions.

When the researcher compared the results from the in-depth interviews to those from the survey of 100 participants, she was surprised to see that talk shows were less preferred in the survey (22 percent) compared to the in-depth interview results (82 percent). Hence, the data from the in-depth interviews could not be validated by the results from the survey. This might be explained by the fact that in the in-depth interviews, the researcher clearly explained what was meant by talk shows, while the quantitative survey did not allow for an explanation. Thus, it was left to the survey participant to understand what was meant by talk shows. This might thus explain

---

[66] Kiran Bedi is India's first female police officer and Magsaysay Award winner.

why 46 percent of the survey participants preferred films as the medium of choice.

Mass media, especially electronic, are the most extensively used media to increase awareness of AIDS and its prevention among the general population in India (IIPS and Macro International -NHFS-3 2005-06; BSS 2006).

As stated above, the majority of people in India are exposed to information about condoms and /or messages about HIV/AIDS via mass media, especially television.

While television is the most known source of information, it is not without limitations. Not only are the televised PSAs (public service announcements) very brief but people watching them normally display a lack of interest toward the information provided to them through PSAs, especially as their risk perception is particularly low. Increased frequency and the duration of AIDS-related information may increase awareness and knowledge among women; however, as Chatterjee (1999) rightly posits in his study on AIDS-related information exposure in India and its influence on women, the information and messages on TV are too brief and impersonal to positively shape their perception on AIDS-related information. Why does television or any other channel source of information not have the expected and desired effect? While messages may indeed be too brief, their duration and the quality of information can easily be improved. However, they may not bear the entire blame for a failure of message reception.

The findings from this study suggest that the majority of women ignored the information provided or did not follow it closely because they were unable to relate to it. Risk perception among almost all of the participants was not just low but virtually nonexistent. As discussed above, condoms are viewed by most as a preventive measure agasint infection rather than as a means of contraception. Low-risk perception is one of the most significant, though not the only, reasons why married Indian couples do not want to use condoms. Thus, most audiences show disinterest in topics such as condoms and HIV/AIDS because they do not believe or want to believe that promiscuity or disease can touch their lives, that is until this "virtual" danger becomes real and imminent and thus personal. It is clear that people have heard about condoms, but it is unclear why they are not listening. The answer may lie in what Rogers (2003) calls "selective exposure"[67]: Individuals consciously or unconsciously avoid messages that are in conflict with their existing predispositions. For example, as seen in the section on barriers to condom use, one of the main reasons for women not asking or wanting to ask their partners to use condom is its deep-seated association with promiscuity which is deep seated in their heart and mind. Hence responses such as,

"On TV, we may have heard but we don't bother with such useless things…"

Rogers uses Hassinger's selective perception theory to further elaborate on this point. Hassinger (Hassinger 1959–cited in Rogers

[67] Defined as, the tendency to interpret communication messages in terms of the individual's existing attitudes and beliefs.

2003) argues that individuals seldom expose themselves to messages about an innovation unless they first feel the need for the innovation, and even if individuals are exposed to innovation messages, such exposure will have little effect unless the innovation is perceived as relevant to the individual's needs and consistent with individual's attitudes and beliefs.

Among other factors (such as low education, socio-economic conditions), women have been known to feel as less empowered to express and/or assess information related to sexual matters (Ghosh et al. 2009). It is common knowledge that most people, including women, are able to discuss day-to-day topics related to sexual reproductive life with their friends and close female relatives like sisters or sisters-in law, and to some extent even mothers and /or mothers-in law. However, this study shows that while topics relating to sex and reproduction may be to some extent a part of conversation among peers, they may hesitate to share very intimate sexual reproductive health problems such as those relating to symptoms relative to infection ranging from minor vaginal infection to STIs. Interestingly, instead of television or close relatives and friends, most married women indicated that doctors are their preferred source for information regarding intimate topics relative to sexual reproductive health, including condoms etc. This preference alludes to women's need for a change agent. The first and foremost role that a change agent has to play is to "develop a need for change". According to Rogers (2003), *"a change agent often initially helps clients become aware of the need to alter their behavior. In order to initiate the innovation-decision process, the change agent points out new alternatives to existing problems, dramatizes the importance of these problems, thereby help create new needs"*. Given that doctors are perceived as credible, trustworthy and competent, their suggestion to the clients that condoms are "the" alternative over other modes of contraception may prove to be highly successful. At the same time, they can use their credibility to change women's personal negative attitude toward condoms (CF.Why are condoms not popular as contraceptives). Since the change agents suggested here are doctors and public health officials, it is recommended that additional health services, other than just condom promotion, be provided to women according their "needs" and "wants". This would be beneficial for the program as it would be easier to create rapport with the women and their families, enabling them to be more receptive and open to the idea of using a condom as a contraceptive.

While the initial focus was on condoms as a key family planning method, the introduction of its "dual positioning" to address HIV prevention was introduced in the late 1980s. A variety of media and other approaches were tried for promotion with interpersonal communication (introducing the "triple protection" positioning, bringing STIs into the conversation on protection). The overall impact of several years of communication was an increase in awareness levels about condoms with respect to their role in preventing both unwanted pregnancies and sexually transmitted infections such as HIV/AIDS. Awareness of their preventive role, the establishment of certain brand identities, building facilitating environments such as freedom from embarrassment during purchase or hesitancy to talk about condoms, have all been attempted. Most have been successful, but the impact on behavior adoption in the context of condom usage has not been commensurate with the efforts made for condom promotion. One of the reasons is that condoms are seen more as preventive agasint STIs, including HIV/AIDS prevention, than as a contraceptive. The findings in this study also point to the stigmatized image of the condom as one of the main reasons for not being popular among the general masses. While NACO understands that to increase condom adoption, its image needs to be normalized (hence the above-mentioned efforts), the organization simultaneously finds low-risk perception to be another major impediment to be overcome. To address this, NACO has prepared communication strategies to increase risk perceptions associated with not using condoms among target groups. The communication has been structured in three levels – to make consumer 'aware' that risks are real, to get him to deliberate on risks versus condom usage and to motivate him to be a consistent user of condoms. NACO gives the following reason for the normalization and risk perception campaign:

"While condom normalisation campaigns helped in gaining social support and promoted desirable beliefs, risk perception campaigns focus purely on the individual's behaviour. So with normalization campaigns, an individual finds much needed encouragement and motivation to win over his social environment, i.e., community, peers and family. In risk perception campaigns, he is motivated to exercise his ability to act and change his behaviour with his responsible actions by using condom. The underlying message of 'triple protection' would run through the communication, not overtly but as

182

a necessary reinforcement, especially for newer audiences that get added to the audience profile every year. Messaging on triple protection forms the by-line of all the campaigns." (NACO 2008)

However, as noted previously[68], while the condom normalization campaign moved straight to promoting it as a "smart man's choice", the past negative image of the condom was not challenged overtly and conclusively. This means that the negative image of the condom and its association with promiscuity and infection might still persist in the minds of audiences, which could partly explain the low impact that condom promotion programs have had on behavior change to date.

As Trout and Al Ries (1986) explain, *"to move a new idea or product into the mind, you must first move an old one out".* According to this notion, once the old idea (in this case, old negative image) is removed, selling the new idea (selling condoms as contraceptives) is often much simpler. *"The crux of a repositioning program is undercutting an existing concept, product... People like to watch the bubble burst."* Condom promoters must change the negative image of condoms, that is, the negative image of condoms must be replaced by something more positive and acceptable.

5.5 Conclusion

This chapter presents the interpretations and discussions of the findings presented in the previous chapter. These findings are

---

[68] P. 49

discussed in conjunction with the existing studies and literature relevant to this research. It was seen that in the context of dealing with the challenge of domestic marital violence, even if women have access to all relevant information, it may still not be enough if their underlying attitudes and beliefs are not supportive of women themselves in the fight against domestic violence including sexual violence. This stems from their tolerant attitudes toward domestic violence, which condone the act and are justified with reasons such as financial dependency, shame and for the sake of the children. What also emerges from the study is that in regard to condom acceptance, intervention programs should also address the need to dissociate the negative image of condoms from promiscuity and disease and to promote it as a healthy means of family planning as well as AIDS prevention.

6 Conclusion, limitations and future research directions

6.1 Conclusion

Indian women's views, beliefs and opinions on domestic violence are skewed more in favor of Indian married men – in favor of husbands rather than of women themselves. The study indicates that the pro-tolerance attitude toward spousal abuse, especially sexual abuse, is deeply entrenched in traditional gender norms. Factors such as shame and the children's sake were seen to strongly influence women's opinions on silently tolerating abuse. This results in a daunting task for those fighting violence against women and seeking to change women's beliefs and views. Changing the beliefs of Indian women is a much needed first step as is changing the views of men toward domestic violence. Violence itself has no place in a domestic setting and is destructive to domestic harmony. It should be as unacceptable for a husband to beat his wife as it is for a wife to beat her husband. In this study, all the women unanimously agreed that a woman should never beat her husband no matter the circumstances. The question then arises as to why it should be acceptable when the roles are reversed. This belief needs to be changed in their minds. Unless a woman respects herself and is ready to take a stand for herself and for other women, she will continue to be exploited and made a victim of senseless domestic violence. Importantly, it also further reinforces gender biased norms permitting and condoning violence against women. With respect to gender equality and women's empowerment in India, Kishor and Gupta argue that *"Agreement with these normatively prescribed powers of men over women reflect an acceptance of unequal gender roles, on the one hand, and a lack of awareness about women's entitlement to bodily security and integrity, on the other. Although such attitudes do not necessarily imply approval of these rights for men, they do signify passive acceptance of norms that give men these rights. Further, widespread acceptance perpetuates such norms and contributes to the low status of women and the girl child* "(Kishor and Gupta, 2009).

It was seen in the research findings that various beliefs and attitudes of women need to be addressed. Even if women are provided with and have access to all relevant information, which to date not the case, it will still prove insufficient if women's underlying attitudes and beliefs are not supportive of women themselves in the fight against domestic violence including sexual violence. The findings indicate that most women prefer to tolerate sexual abuse silently, with only a small percentage preferring to seek family intervention; thus, this study highlights the need to: firstly, change women's attitude, for instance, by addressing them specifically, especially through media campaigns, and communicating that violence is unacceptable and is not a matter of shame. Ellsberg et al. (2001) posit that such media campaigns are likely to have a positive influence on women who are subject to domestic violence.

Changing women's pro-tolerance beliefs and strengthening their belief in their own personal self-efficacy become more crucial as there are rarely witnesses or by-standers in cases of sexual violence. While no distinction in perception was made between unsafe sex and unwanted sex, a larger percentage (38 percent) of married women participants prefer to seek help from a family member if they perceive themselves to be at risk. This finding strongly highlights the need to strengthen the community network in order to involve them in the fight against domestic violence and design messages to help the victims of DV to get the legal and/or medical support they need. In other words, strong social safety networks must also be created for women so that they can seek support, solace and help when they are victimized. These networks will embolden women to take a stand favoring themselves and to come forward for their own safety and for other women. They also need to be made aware of such safety networks as well as the laws which have been enacted to combat domestic violence. As seen in Chapter two, the existing socio-legal support network in India must be further strengthened. However, any awareness of such networks will be of no use unless women change their view of domestic violence and they are provided with a strong social safety net. According to Heise and Elias (1995), strategic interventions to fight domestic violence should involve fighting the cultural beliefs and biases that denigrate women and helping women organize on their own behalf. They further argue that unless women have power equal to that of men, they will remain at a heightened risk of AIDS (Heise and Elias 1995).

Additionally, the existing literature shows that perpetrating partners of abused women are more likely to engage in high-risk behavior, thereby making them more vulnerable to HIV infection. It is thus crucial for communication interventions to target the wives of abusive husbands. However, this is not a goal easily achieved. As pointed out by women participants in this research, wives may often be unaware or ignorant of their husband's high-risk activities, especially extramarital relations. This may also include men those who are MSMs (Solomon et al. 2010) or those having extramarital sex, including frequenting FSWs (Schensul et al. 2006). A starting point, for instance, could be the targeting of, for instance, wives of alcoholic husbands or IDUs as research has found positive associations between DV, alcohol and substance abuse and an increased risk of HIV. As seen in the study by Solomon et al (2010) , this married group may be more aware of their husband's high-risk behavior and, will be able to better help themselves if they are provided with appropriate information and support.

The contribution of this research to the literature on domestic violence and HIV is three fold. Firstly, the findings from this study show that married women's awareness and knowledge about the legal support system is almost negligent. Secondly, a majority of participants did not acknowledge forced sex as marital rape. Finally, it reveals the opinions of married women in regard to coping strategies in cases of sexual violence, including forced unsafe sex. Based on the interviews conducted, this study shows that unsafe sex was not seen as any different from unwanted sex. Interestingly, interviews with women participants showed that although they resign themselves to forced unsafe sex and tolerate it silently under "normal circumstances", they would not easily subject themselves to forced sex without a condom if they were aware of their husband's HIV status or their high-risk sex behavior, neither of which is easily known.

Gender inequality, a tolerant attitude toward the husband subjecting his wife to physical and or sexual violence, lack of a woman's autonomy regarding her sexual and reproductive health choices have their roots firmly entrenched in traditional unequal gender norms. One might ask oneself whether married couples would use condoms more (than is now the case) if there is an equal gender power equation within marital relations. This may not be necessarily true. Firstly, changing gender norms might render conditions more favorable for women to negotiate condom use but would not address the issue of acceptability. Secondly, changing deeply entrenched traditional gender norms is a difficult and lengthy process and changing a particular thought or belief will take more than one generation, while changing norms will take even longer.

This led the researcher to probe more deeply into women's perceptions regarding condom use and factors inhibiting the use of condoms within a marital relationship. The findings revealed that one of the major reasons for the unacceptability of condoms is their negative association with infection, promiscuity and lack of trust within a relationship. This finding supports previous studies on barriers to condom use (Joseph Roth, Krishnan, and Bunch 2001; Bhattacharya 2004) and also references women's fear and reluctance to negotiate condom use. This study expands on the literature by showing that apart from the social stigma attached to condoms, the reproductive life and later female sterilization represent two other major obstacles to condom usage among married couples. As Rogers aptly points out, *"Individuals do not always recognize when they have a problem, and the individual's perceived needs may not agree with what experts think the individuals need." (Rogers, diffusion of innovation)*

In other words, married people do not feel the need for condom use because, firstly, they do not believe themselves to be at risk and secondly, because they either they to conceive or have completed their family and opted for permanent sterilization. Condom negotiation among couples is often an emotionally charged topic. We need to address the fears that are deeply embedded in the hearts of most married women, for instance, the fear of one's partner becoming violent or angry if asked to use a condom or the fear of mistrusting or being mistrusted by one's partner etc. (Go et al, 2003).

This study indicates the need to normalize the image of condoms and, in marketing terms, "reposition" them, which is possible by firstly, dissociating the negative image of condom from promiscuity and disease and secondly, creating a need for condoms. The latter can be accomplished by understanding the married couple's needs that have not been met or satisfied by other contraceptives. The many benefits of condoms such as ease of use, reliability, easy availability and almost no side effects need to be strongly emphasized. Compared to its bigger competitor in the market of contraceptives, sterilization, which is permanent and non-reversible, condoms are safer and more convenient and they provide a dual benefit of preventing pregnancies as well as STDs such as HIV/AIDS. Sterilization is merely a contraceptive and does not prevent STDs. This benefit of condoms may not be overtly emphasized, but once condoms are acceptable, this goal could also be achieved. The dual goals of contraception as well as AIDS prevention can be met with one product. Hence, it is very important to properly position and propagate condom use. By promoting it more as a convenient contraceptive for married couples increased condom use would also meet the aim of preventing vulnerable married women from becoming infected with STDs. Increasing condom acceptance may also end the negotiation dilemma that married women are known to face. While this would be an underlying, and not an overtly promoted benefit, it would be an equally important and useful one. HIV prevention can be the aim of the program but, its marketing strategy should be through the promotion of condoms as a better means of contraception in order to make them more acceptable and decrease hesitation or avoid dilemmas in the minds of the target group, in particular, heterosexual married couples.

Another important finding was that the majority of women prefer that their husbands decide which contraceptive to use, especially whether to use a condom or not. This highlights the need to involve men in family planning. Emphasizing their roles and responsibilities in regard to family welfare and reproductive health is one of the critical success factors not only for family planning but also for selling condoms.

Involving men in the contraception and sexual health decision-making process is not a particularly novel idea and has been used in several projects worldwide. For example, a three-year male motivation project was initiated by the Zimbabwe National Family Planning Council (ZNFPC) in 1988. A survey conducted after the entertainment-educational program revealed that not only were the men who were exposed to the project more likely to mention modern family planning methods, but they were also more likely to use such methods. Current use of any modern method, particularly condoms, was significantly greater among men exposed to the campaign than men who were not (Piotrow and Kincaid et al. 1992).

Though not exhaustive, this study provides insights into the needs and wants of women regarding the information they require and the channels through which they would like to receive that information. In this respect two points came to light: Firstly, the information regarding the DV Act 2005, including the specific services it stipulates, is almost negligible. During the in-depth interviews, married women expressed their preference for talk shows as a venue for addressing the issue on a societal level. This venue provides a platform for the unheard voices and valuable information through the experts who guide and mediate the conversation. While the response to talk shows was observed to be highly positive during the interviews, the survey data could not validate the information generated from the interviews (see Chapter 5.4, pp 125). Further research intervention is required to confirm married women's opinions on this issue. Also, most women participants reported an inability to relate to the television information given on the television to the term regarding HIV/AIDS and condoms due to the negative association with and a perceived lack of need for condoms. Finally this study indicates women's need for a change agent, preferably a doctor, to provide more information regarding intimate topics concerning sexual reproductive health, including HIV/AIDS and condoms. Further research is required to assess and confirm these needs.

To the researcher's knowledge, this is the first qualitative study of its kind to reveal in women's own words their perception and attitudes toward marital violence, including marital rape and forced unsafe sex. It also revealed that while fear of violence prevails, women did not express a need to use condoms as a result of the negative relationship between condoms and trust. Consistent with other studies, this study brings three main reasons for low condom usage to light – firstly, wanting to conceive; secondly, opting for female sterilization after having the desired number of children; and finally, the negative associations surrounding condoms.

6.2 Limitations & Strengths

6.2.1 Limitations

This research has some limitations:

- The present study is based on Indian married women who live in or around an urban slum in Mumbai, a metropolis in Western India. Given the limitation of the sample size to an urban slum population, this study may not be not generalizable to other populations such as rural married women, middle or high income urban women, or rich educated married women.

- Given the sensitivity of the topics discussed, sexual violence, sexual behavior, condom use etc., there may be reporting bias. However, all participants were assured of confidentiality, i.e., that their name and identity would not be revealed. All women participants were informed about the sensitivity of the subject beforehand to minimize the incidence of shock or discomfort. Also, the researcher (a woman herself) personally conducted all face-to-face interviews and ensured that women participants felt comfortable and did not feel intimidated in any way. Additionally, to further counter reporting bias, the responses emerging from the qualitative data were further validated by a quantitative survey with 100 additional married women belonging to the same demographic.

- This study limits its focus to violence and condom use within marriage. Hence, it does not represent intimate partner violence

194

or condom use outside marriage, such as in premarital, extramarital, and commercial relationships.

- Moreover, this research limits its scope to the study of acceptability and (non) use of male condoms within marriage and does not include the acceptance of female condoms and microbicides. It should be noted however that female condoms and microbicides are still new and largely unknown to our study demographic.

6.2.2 Strengths

Despite these limitations, the key strength of this study is that it provides rich qualitative data on sensitive topics such as domestic marital physical and sexual violence and condom acceptability, expressed through married women's own words. It also presents the individual perspective as well as the opinions, beliefs, and attitudes of the participants, all of whom live in metropolitan urban slum areas.

6.3   Future research directions:

6.3.1   Future research methods may include additional in–depth qualitative interviews as well as quantitative studies. Areas of further investigation may include (in both quantitative and qualitative intervention) the attitude perception of wives of high-risk practicing men on tolerating physical and/or sexual violence, how they cope with violence (if they have been a victim themselves), understanding their perspective on sexual reproductive rights, their strengths and weaknesses in protecting themselves and their children, analyzing their existing support network and how it can be strengthened. Also, study samples could include wives of members of high-risk groups, especially those men who are more easily identifiable such as, IDUs, alcoholics).

6.3.2   Further investigation is needed to assess married women's preferences regarding the nature of inform.ation, channels of information, identifying and designing messages emerging from such studies as well as those from point 6.3.1.

6.3.3   Future studies could explore couple's perspectives on accepting condoms as a means of family planning and analyze the strengths and weaknesses of condom promotion programs compared to sterilization as a main competitor to condoms in the field of family planning. Could Family planning hold one of the master keys to win the battle against HIV/AIDS in India?

6.3.4   Studies might focus on Indian men's perspectives on, motivation for and involvement in family planning programs

6.3.5   Any combination of the above

While this research has generated findings that enrich the existing body of knowledge with regards to women's perspectives towards issues like domestic violence and condom acceptability, further research along the lines described above above would be invaluable in extending this body of knowledge and lead to greater benefit by generating additional data and ensuring the applicability of the study in practice.

7 Appendix I - Target Audience Assessment Questionnaire

- **Target Audience Assessment Questionnaire**

The researcher introduces herself to the interviewee, tells him/her about the research objective – why she is doing the research, what is the purpose of the research, and how they can help tell the interviewee that the researcher want to know their side of the story and understand his/her perspective on the issue and how is it so significant for the research.

INFORMED CONSENT

Hello. My name is Rachna Talwar and I am doing Doctoral studies at University of St. Gallen, Switzerland. I am conducting a survey and in depth interview to ask men and women about their needs of communication for issues such as sexual reproductive health etc.. I would very much appreciate your participation in this interview. This information will help to plan better communication strategies for women and men (so as to impart more information, better messages and effective channels to impart those messages). The survey usually

---

takes about 20 minutes to complete.

Whatever information you provide will be kept strictly confidential and will not be shown to other persons.

Participation in this survey is voluntary, and if we should come to any question you don't want to answer, just let me know and I will go on to the next question; or you can stop the interview at any time. However, we hope that you will participate in this survey since your views are important.

At this time, do you want to ask me anything about the survey?

May I begin the interview now?

Signature of interviewer: Date:

RESPONDENT AGREES TO BE INTERVIEWED . . . . (Signature)

Introductory (demographic profile) &Warm up Comfort questions -

Name	
Age	
Sex	
Education	
Occupation	
Religion	
Region (where are they from etc.)	

Other misc. questions:

How many children do they have? How old are they? Their education?

Who else lives with them in the same house?

Now I would like to ask you questions about some other important aspects of a woman's life. I know that some of these questions are very personal. However, your answers are crucial for helping to understand the condition of women in [COUNTRY]. Let me assure you that your answers are completely confidential and will not be told to anyone and no one else will know that you were asked these questions.

Who in your family usually has the final say on the following decisions :	HUSBAND/PARTNER=2 RESPONDENT&HUSBAND/PARTNER JOINTLY=3 SOMEONEELSE=4 RESPONDENT&SOMEONEELSE

Whether or not you should work to earn money? Whether or not to use a method to avoid having children?	JOINTLY=5 DECISION NOT MADE /NOT APPLICABLE=6 WORK . . . . . 1 2 3 4 5 6 METHOD . . . 1 2 3 4 5 6
Who in your family usually has the final say the following decisions:	HUSBAND/PARTNER=2 RESPONDENT&HUSBAND/PARTNER JOINTLY=3 SOMEONEELSE=4 RESPONDENT&SOMEONEELSE JOINTLY=5 DECISION NOT MADE /NOT APPLICABLE=6
Whether to have another child?	OTHER CHILD......... 1 2 3 4 5 6
Now I would like to get your opinion on some aspects of family life.	

Please tell me if you agree or disagree with each statement:			
a) The important decisions in the family should be made only by the men of the family.	Agree 1	Disagree 2	Don't Know 3
FAMILY DECISIONS BY MEN	Agree 1	Disagree 2	Don't Know 3
The wife has a right to express her opinion even when she disagrees with what her husband is saying.	Agree 1	Disagree 2	Don't Know 3
WIFE TO EXPRESS OPINION	Agree 1	Disagree 2	Don't Know 3
A wife should tolerate being beaten by her husband in order to keep	Agree 1	Disagree 2	Don't Know 3

the family together. TOLERATE BEING BEATEN			
A wife should tolerate being sexually abused by her husband in order to keep the family together TOLERATE BEING SEXUALLY ABUSED	Agree 1	Disagree 2	Don't Know 3
If a wife is forced to sex by her husband, is it rape?	Agree 1	Disagree 2	Don't Know 3

Asked after opinion questions

Q1. What should be a wife's role in decision making about: contraception; sex; going to doctor in case of sexual reproductive health problem

-   Can/ should a woman decide if to use a condom or not? Why /why not?

If she has sex related issues, who does she/should she discuss it with? Who she does not feel free to discuss it with?

- How does she feel going to a doctor /discussing it with Doctor? (Have they ever discussed those issues /taken treatment / counsel for those issues?

- What does their husband feel about discussing these issues outside?

Q2. Do you believe a woman should be dominated by her husband?

Q3. What should a woman do /react/behave if her husband forces her to have?

- Unwanted sex –

- Unsafe sex –

- Does not let her go to the doctor even if she has a sexual reproductive health problem

Q4. Who should dominate who in – marriage; sex life?

Q5. Do you think a wife should beat her husband? Do you think a husband should beat his wife? Under what circumstances do u think is it OK for a husband to beat his wife?

Q6. Is it OK for a husband to force wife for sex? Do you believe that Rape within marriage exists?

205

Q7. What case have you heard about DV?

Now if you will permit me, I need to ask some more questions about your relationship with your (last) husband/partner. If we should come to any question that you do not want to answer, just let me know and we will go on to the next question.

Sexual Relationship Power Scale A Relationship Control Subscale				
1. If I asked my partner to use a condom, he would get violent.	Strongly Agree Disagree.	Agree	Disagree	Strongly
	1	2	3	4
2. If I asked my partner to use a condom, he would get angry.				
	1	2	3	4
3. Most of the time, we do what my partner wants to do.				
4. My partner won't let me wear certain things.				
	1	2	3	4
5. When my partner and				

I are together, I'm pretty quiet.	1	2	3	4
6. My partner has more say than I do about important decisions that affect us.				
7. My partner tells me who I can spend time with.	1	2	3	4
8. If I asked my partner to use a condom, he would think I'm having sex with other people.	1	2	3	4
9. I feel trapped or stuck in our relationship.	1	2	3	4
10. My partner does what he wants, even if I do not want him to.	1	2	3	4
11. I am more committed to our relationship than my partner is.				
12. When my partner	1	2	3	4

and I disagree, he gets his way most of the time.	1	2	3	4
13. My partner gets more out of our relationship than I do.	Strongly Agree Disagree.	Agree	Disagree	Strongly
	1	2	3	4
14. My partner always wants to know where I am.				
15. My partner might be having sex with someone else.	1	2	3	4
Decision-Making Dominance Subscale				
16. Who usually has more say about whose friends to go out with?	1	2	3	4
17. Who usually has more say about whether you have sex?	1	2	3	4
18. Who usually has more say about what	1	2	3	4

you do together?				
19. Who usually has more say about how often you see one another?	Strongly Agree Disagree.	Agree	Disagree	Strongly
	1	2	3	4
20. Who usually has more say about when you talk about serious things?	1	2	3	4
21. In general, who do you think has more power in your relationship?				
	1	2	3	4
22. Who usually has more say about whether you use condoms? Does not use condom , don't know who will decide	1	2	3	4
23. Who usually has more say about what types of sexual acts you				

	1	2	3	4
do				
24. I have sex if my partner wants me to, even if I don't want to				
25. I refuse to have sex if I don't want to, even if my partner ins ists.(Pregancy-STD Prevention)	1	2	3	4
26. I have sex without a condom or latex barrier if my partner doesn't like them, even if I want to use one.	1	2	3	4
27. I have sex without using a condom or latex barrier if my partner insists, even if I don't want to.	1	2	3	4
	1	2	3	4

	1 2 3 4
	Strongly Agree Agree Disagree Strongly Disagree.
	1 2 3 4
	1 2 3 4
Domestic violence (Does/did) your (last) husband/partner ever do	**(If yes, How often did this happen during the last 12 months: often, only sometimes, or not at all?)**

any of the following things to you:				
a) Push you, shake you, or throw something at you?		Often	Sometimes	Not at all
	Yes	1	2	3
	No			
b) Slap you?				
c) Punch you with his fist or with something that could hurt you?	Yes	1	2	3
	No			
	Yes	1	2	3
	No			
d) Threaten or attack you with a knife, gun, and any other weapon?				
	Yes	1	2	3
	No			
e) Physically force you to have sexual				

	intercourse with him even when you did not want to?			
	Yes	1	2	3
	No			
f)	Physically force you to have sexual intercourse with him without condom even when you did not want to?			
	Yes	1	2	3
	No			
g)	Force you to perform any sexual acts you did not want to?			

	Yes 1 2 3 No
Does (did) your husband/partner drink alcohol?	YES . . . . 1 NO 2
How often does (did) he get drunk: often, only sometimes, or never?	OFTEN. . . . . .1 OFTEN . . . . 1 SOMETIMES . . . . 2 NEVER 3

Have you heard about HIV/AIDS?	Yes, If yes, from where have you heard about it? No
Have you heard about DV Act 2005?	Yes, If yes, from where have you heard about it? No
Have you heard about any hotline number for victims of DV? 1298, 103	Yes No

Other questions asked during the in- depth interview

Q1. Their experience of DV – know how, awareness and beliefs, values

Q2. Their experience of HIV/AIDS – know how, awareness and beliefs, values

Q3. What communication can do to help their case –

Q4. What communication messages can help?

Q5. What communication mediums do they regularly listen to?

Q6. If behavior has to change what needs to be communicated? What should be contained in the messages?

Q7. Awareness about DV act 2005 and legal services available?

Q8. Who can be the change agents?

8   Appendix II - Follow-up questionnaire

- **Follow-up   questionnaire   (administered   to   100   participants)**

- **Introductory   (demographic   profile)   &Warm   up   Comfort questions -**

Name	
Age	
Sex	
Education	
Occupation	
Religion	

Region (where are they from etc.)	
Other misc. questions: How many children do they have? How old are they?	

Q. Have you heard about condom?	A)Yes B) No
Q. If yes, from where did you hear about condom?	A)TV ; B) Radio; C)Doctor/hospital ; D) from a friend; E) From a relative; F)

	Someone or somewhere else
Q. Have you heard about HIV/AIDS?	A) Yes B) No
Q. If yes, from where did you hear about condom?	A)TV ; B) Radio; C)Doctor/hospital ; D) from a friend; E) From a relative; F) Someone or somewhere else
Q. What should a wife do in case her husband physically forces her for sex?	A)do nothing and tolerate silently ; B)tell an adult in the family ; C)Call the police ; D)Leave husband; E) Do Something else (specify)
Q. If she has sex related issues, who does she/should she discuss it with?	A)Husband; B) Doctor; C)Mother; D)Sister; E)Friend; F)Someone else
Q. Do you use condom?	A)Yes B) No
Q. If yes, what do you like most about using condom? If you do not use condom, why not?	A) Do not know how to use condom; B) Do not know about condom; C) Condom disgusts me; D)Husband does not like to use condom; E)Condom is only for those people who are infected with STD s or HIVetc. F) Condom is only for those people

	who go out /promiscuous
Q.Who should have more say in sex life?	A) Husband B) Wife C) Both
Q.Who has more say in sex life?	A) Husband B) Wife C) Both
Q. Who Should have more say whether to use condom or not?	A) Husband B) Wife C) Both
Q. Who has more say whether to use condom or not?	A) Husband B) Wife C) Both
Q. If I asked my partner to use a condom, he would get violent.	A) Agree B) Disagree
Q. If I asked my partner to use a condom, he would get angry.	A) Agree B) Disagree
Q. If I asked my partner to use a condom, he would think that I don't trust him.	A) Agree B) Disagree
Q. If I asked my partner to use a condom, he would think I'm having sex with other	A) Agree B) Disagree

people.	
Q. How would you like to get information about private intimate stuff, like condom usage, personal body, etc.?	A) TV; B) Radio; C)Doctor ; D) Hospital; E) Friend; F) Relative
Q. how would they like that an issue like DV be addressed via TV?	A)Film ; B) Serial ; C)Talkshow ; D)Some other type of program(please specify)

9 Appendix III – Quantitative Survey* – Data at a glance

Questions
    *(100 Respondents)

1	Age	Average		32 Years	

2	Education	Illiterate		1-6 Class	7 & Higher Class
		24		7	69

3	Occupation	Housewives	Employed
		82	18

4	Have you heard about condoms?	Yes	No
		82	18

5	From where have you heard about condoms?	Doctor / Hospital	TV	Friend / Relative	No Answer
		42	36	10	12

6	Have you heard about HIV/AIDS?	Yes	No
		87	13

7	From where have you heard about HIV/AIDS?	Doctor / Hospital	TV	Friend / Relative	No Answer
		49	37	3	11

8	What should a wife do in case her husband physically forces her for sex?	A: do nothing and tolerate silently	B: tell an adult in the family	C: Call the police	D: Leave husband	E: Do Something else
		62	32	6		

221

9	If she has sex related issues, who does she/should she discuss it with?	A: Husband	B: Doctor	C: Mother	D: Sister	E: Friend
		13	69	3		15

10	Do you use condoms?	Yes		No		No Answer
		25		75		

11	If you do not use condom, why not?	B: Do not know about condoms	C: Condoms disgust me	D: Husband does not like to use condoms	E: Condoms are only for those people who are infected with STDs or HIV etc.	F: Condoms are only for those people who go out /promiscuous
		10	1	24	24	41

12	If I asked my partner to use a condom, he would get violent.	Agree (of 75 respondents who do not use condom)		Disagree(of 75 respondents who do not use condom)		No Answer(75 responde who do use condom
		67		7		1

13	If I asked my partner to use a condom, he would get angry.	Agree(of 75 respondents who do not use condom)		Disagree(of 75 respondents who do not use condom)		No Answer(respond who do use conc
		64		10		1

| 14 | If I asked my partner to use a | Agree(of 75 respondents who | | Disagree(of 75 respondents who | | No Answer(|

condom, he would think that I don't trust him.	do not use condom)	do not use condom)	respond who do use conc
	59	14	2

15	If I asked my partner to use a condom, he would think I'm having sex with other people.	Agree(of 75 respondents who do not use condom)	Disagree(of 75 respondents who do not use condom)	No Answer(respond who do use conc
		52	21	2

16	How would she like to get information about private intimate stuff , like condom usage, personal body , etc. TV, radio or would she prefer that someone like me or a doctor comes to their house to explain...?	Doctor / Hospital	Hospit al	TV	Radio	Nc Ans er
		46	15	33	4	2

17	How would they like that an issues like DV be addressed via TV; movie, serial or a talk show (face to face ....) where on one hand	Serials and Films	Films	Serials	Talk Show	Nc An we
		4	46	26	22	2

people come with their real issues and talk to authorities like police, NGOs, counselors who in turn try to offer solutions as well as try to address their problems?

18 Who should have more say in sex life?	Husband	Wife	Both
	95	1	4

19 Who has more say about sex life in real?	Husband	Wife	Both
	90	6	4

20 Who Should have more say whether to use condom or not?	Husband	Wife	Both
	95	1	4

21 Who has more say about condom use in real?	Husband	Wife	Both
	91	3	6

22 What should a wife do in case her husband physically forces her for unsafe sex?	Tolerate silently	Can talk to elders	Can talk to police	Leave husband
	51	38	7	4

10 Appendix IV - NHFS data

The NHFS data on domestic violence, condom use and HIV Prevalence (Table.6.1), when compared together shows that all the High HIV prevalent states are not only high on domestic violence but also low on condom use. Even more interestingly, the emerging pockets of increasing HIV prevalence also show high domestic violence rate and low condom use.

Table 6.1(a) Data comparing Domestic violence, condom use and HIV prevalence within High HIV prevalent states

High HIV Prevalent States	Domestic violence (physical or sexual violence) (%)	Condom use (%)	HIV Prevalence among women (%)	HIV Prevalence among women and men (%)
Andhra Pradesh	35.2	0.5	0.75	0.97
Karnataka	20	1.7	0.54	0.69
Maharashtra	30.7	6.2	0.48	0.62
Manipur	43.8	4.1	0.76	1.13
Tamil Nadu	41.9	2.3	0.39	0.34

Table 6.2(b) Data comparing Domestic violence, condom use and HIV prevalence within "emerging pockets" of increasing HIV prevalence among low and moderate HIV prevalent states

Low and Moderate HIV Prevalent States	Domestic violence (physical or sexual violence)	Condom use	HIV Prevalence among women	HIV Prevalence among women and men
Gujarat	27.6	5.8	na	
Rajasthan	46.3	5.7	na	
Orissa	38.4	3.0	na	
Uttar Pradesh	59.0	8.6	0.05	0.07
Bihar	42.4	2.3	na	
West Bengal	40.3	4.3	na	

Source: International Institute for Population Sciences (IIPS) and Macro International Inc. Calverton, DHS, India 2005-06 - Final Report (English), Chapters – 05- Family Planning; 12- HIV Prevalence and 15 Domestic violence, Maryland, USA, 2007

11 Appendix V - Excerpts from the fourth Monitoring & Evaluation Report 2010 on the Protection of Women from Domestic Violence Act, 2005

Excerpts from the fourth Monitoring & Evaluation Report 2010 on the Protection of Women from Domestic Violence Act, 2005

1) Prior to the enactment of the Protection of Women from Domestic Violence Act, 2005 (PWDVA) in India, domestic violence was addressed through Section 498 A of the Indian Penal Code, 1860 (IPC). Under Section 498 A, physical or mental cruelty to the wife by the husband or his relatives was made a cognizable and non-bailable offense punishable with imprisonment up to three years and fi ne. Subsequently, Section 304B was introduced in the IPC in 1986 which created a new offence of "dowry death".

While criminal law provides for prosecution of perpetrators, it does not take into account the woman's immediate needs of protection, shelter and monetary relief. Also, criminal law alone does not fully recognise the responsibility of the state towards the victims of violence. On the other hand, existing civil law remedies of divorce and maintenance were unable to provide effective reliefs to women facing violence and the proceedings under the civil law were time consuming. Even when injunction orders were available, the enforcement of the same was weak due to absence of penalties for violation.

2) The Act places specifi c onus on the central and state governments to provide appropriate infrastructure for the effective implementation of the Act.(Section 11, PWDVA, 2005.)

3) Stakeholders under PWDA

- Protection Officers
- Service Providers
- Medical Facilities and Shelter Homes

Several gaps have been identified in regards to infrastructure for effective implementation of the Act. Firstly, lack of sufficient and proper access of women to Protection officer (PO). The latest M&E Report also recommends the need for a dedicated cadre of POs that would be sensitive to the women, and guide and support them through the pre-litigation process. As per the report, women have little knowledge of the existence of the POs. It was also noticed that Lawyer remains the key stakeholder for the PWDVA. Women approach private lawyers directly and legal aid services through the POs or SPs. However, mostly, their experience with the lawyers was negative. It was marked by delays, corruption, and frequent change of lawyers.

Another major point raised by the M&E report is that enforcement of orders and reporting of breach continue to be a challenge., Women from some of the states reported that that the orders were

not being followed up, and they had complained to the court, Police and the PO.

"Restrictions have been placed on my husband's movements. He cannot come here (where my parents live) but he drinks and comes here often and creates nuisance. No, the Police do not do anything- I think they are hand in glove with him. " Woman, 27 years, Jodhpur

"I got residence and protection order. The order could not be enforced as my in-laws created hurdles for me each time. My advocate had fi led an application for non-compliance of the order. Enforcement of the order is a real challenge. " Woman, 32 years, Delhi

The woman doesn't get protection the way she expects. We have experienced it many times that the order is received and still the woman is beaten. There is no use of the PO. In very few cases has the AP felt the advantage of receiving a PO. The orders remain on paper. The woman does not get protection. She has to stay there forcefully. She doesn't get the Police protection she needs. PO, Mumbai

A low level of awareness among key stakeholders has been an issue since the first year of implementation. The latest M&E report shows that this issue is still a matter of concern. The representatives from different states were in agreement that intensive trainings needed to be held for all the stakeholders including the Judiciary and also health professionals. It has been reiterated that the

4)   The PO acts as a link between the women, the courts and all the other stakeholders under the PWDVA. Therefore, the role of the PO consists of various functions, inter alia submission of the DIR, service of notice, and enforcement of orders.

5) *Police remains the first point of contact for more than half of the women. Only a few police personnel who had received training had knowledge of the key provisions of the Act but they too were unclear about their specific roles. Further, they had not shared the information with their peers at the police station.*

6) *Police inaction in case of breach of protection order presumably due to the lack of understanding and awareness of the law among the stakeholders and Police, also was indicative of breach not being reported at all, or no action taken by police.*

State Judicial Academies and Police Academies should step up their gender sensitization trainings on the PWDVA.

Interestingly, budget allocation shows a different picture altogether. While the M&E report has been pointing out the need for training of key stakeholders. Some of the states , if not all , showed either no expenditure incurred despite budget allocation to "gender sensitization programs" or fund allocation itself has been not been a sustained exercise. On the other hand, while many states have provided funds for the training of POs, all other agencies and individuals involved in the implementation of the Act such as the Medical Officers, police personnel, Magistrates and SPs also need adequate information about the Act. Lack of proper training and

information has also been one of the major reasons for improper co ordination among various stakeholders, which consequently raises question on efficiency of implementation of the PWDVA Act. As per the Mid-Term Appraisal of the Eleventh Five Year Plan (2010)ii,66 the PWDVA has been unable to reach the intended beneficiaries owing to lack of information and mechanisms for its enforcement. Lack of financial provisions by the central government to the state governments for its enforcement was one of the major factors of concerns expressed by The CEDAW Committee in its Concluding Comments (2007-09).

Another component that has not received sufficient attention is the support for the SPs (shelter provisions) notified under the Act. As noted in the first part of this chapter, most of the states have notified existing SHs (shelter homes)run under 'Swadhar' scheme or Nari Niketans. Swadhar is a central government scheme, which gives grants to the states to set up SHs for women in distress. The report of the Centre for Budget and Governance Accountability, 2010iii highlights that Swadhar scheme has consistently recorded Actual Expenditures higher than the Budget Estimates and Revised Estimates. This reflects a huge demand for such a scheme. Quite contrary to this, the output data of the annual report of the MWCD (2008-09) reveals that there were only 287 Swadhar shelter homes operational across the country, which means there is not even one per district. Given that the average population per district is more than 15 lakh, this is extremely inadequate. With the introduction of the PWDVA and notification of Swadhar shelter homes as SPs, it is all the more important that adequate number of such homes be constructed and quality of services is ensured.

In short, the M&E report points out that while some states have initiated action with respect to providing resources for the implementation of the PWDVA several problems remain. There has been no allocation made for the specific components of the Act, and even when allocations have been made they have not been fully utilised. Worse still, there are many states that have not committed any resources for the PWDVA. They claim that the existing women welfare programs will be sufficient to fulfill the provisions under the Act.

After 5 years if implementation, most women are unaware of existence of DV Act 2005, any very few would know of PO as their first point of contact. Hence, in case of need, majority would approach the police directly. While lack of awareness about the law and its provisions for the benefit of women victims of domestic violence is one problem, their negative experience of interaction with police is a bigger problem and major put off for most women.

When women reach out for help, the nearest police station is the most familiar place to approach. However, often, the women were unable to register a complaint and met with insensitive behaviour. Police did not perceive intervening in the family as their responsibility and usually advise women to adjust and return home. Also, many were quick to judge the woman. Complaints of bribery and corruption also ran through these narratives, as is evident from the quote below. Some women reported that initially the Police would call their husbands to threaten them and settle the matter, but brushed the women off on subsequent visits. In some cases even PO's were known to judge the women or advice them to reconcile with their husbands.

"First I make her sit and tell me the whole account patiently. Then when I feel that she has actually faced violence, I try and explain to her to agree to a compromise. I also talk to her marital family members. If I feel that the problem is not that much, then I advise her not to proceed with filling the DIR. If I feel that there is no scope for compromise, or the women is really facing brutal violence, then I inform her about the process under the PWDVA in detail and fill the DIR. We ensure that only after both the parties don't reach a compromise that we fill the DIR."

PO, Jaipur

In another case, the PO believed that the woman who came to her for filling the DIR had not made enough efforts to adjust in the husband's family. The PO advised her to go back and ask for 'forgiveness' from her husband.

This indicates that the PO's intervention to save the marriage at all costs is diametrically opposed to the spirit of the PWDVA.

This once again points to the urgent need for not only for increased and comprehensive information and training regarding PWDVA but also to provide ongoing training particularly on gender power imbalances, marriage as a social institution, and its impact on women.

Negative, judgmental and gender insensitive attitude has been noticed to be a major barrier to women's access to law. Personal, witnessed or mere listening to other people's negative experiences would make women victims hesitate to seek help in future.

Apart from enforcement of Act in terms of protection and maintenance as being a major challenge, another major issue of concern is reluctance on part of the judges to take serious note of sexual violence.

Source: "Staying Alive", Fourth Monitoring & Evaluation Report 2010 on the Protection of Women from Domestic Violence Act, 2005, Lawyers Collective Women's Rights Initiative and International Center for Research on Women, 2010. Accessed November 2011

http://www.unwomensouthasia.org/assets/LCWRI-4th-PWDVA-ME-Report-2010-Staying-Alive3.pdf

12 References

Ackermann, Leáne, and Gerhardt W. de Klerk. "Social factors that make South African women vulnerable to HIV infection." Health care for women international 23, no. 2 (2002): 163-172.doi: 10.1080/073993302753429031.

Airhihenbuwa, Collins O., and Rafael Obregon. "A critical assessment of theories/models used in health communication for HIV/AIDS." Journal of health communication 5, no. S1 (2000): 5-15.doi: 10.1080/10810730050019528.

Ali, Mohamed M., John Cleland, and Iqbal H. Shah. "Condom use within marriage: a neglected HIV intervention." Bulletin of the World Health Organization 82, no. 3 (2004): 180-186.doi: /10.1590/S0042-96862004000300007.

Amin Avni. "Comment - India's AIDS control programme." The Great Game, Seminar 527, July 2003.

Babu Bontha, and Shantanu Kar. "Domestic violence against women in eastern India: a population-based study on prevalence and related issues." BMC Public Health 9, no. 1 (2009): 129. doi: 10.1186/1471-2458-9-129.

Bajwa, Sukhwinder Kaur, Sukhminder Jit Singh Bajwa, Gagandeep Kaur Ghai, Kamaljit Singh, and Nirankar Singh. "Knowledge, attitudes, beliefs, and perception of the North Indian population toward adoption of contraceptive practices." Asia-Pacific Journal of Public Health (2011).doi: 10.1177/1010539511411473.

Balaiah, D., D. D. Naik, R. C. Parida, M. Ghule, K. T. Hazari, and H. S. Juneja. "Contraceptive knowledge, attitude and practices of men in rural Maharashtra." Advances in contraception 15, no. 3 (1999): 217-234.doi: 10.1023/A:1006753617161

Bandura, Albert. "Perceived self-efficacy in the exercise of control over AIDS infection." Evaluation and program planning 13, no. 1 (1990): 9-17.doi: 10.1016/0149-7189(90)90004-G.

Bandura, Albert. "Social cognitive theory and exercise of control over HIV infection." Preventing AIDS: Theories and methods of behavioral interventions (1994): 25-59.

Bandura, Albert. "Social cognitive theory for personal and social change by enabling media." Entertainment-education and social change: History, research, and practice (2004): 75-96.

Bandura, Albert. "Social cognitive theory in cultural context." Applied Psychology 51, no. 2 (2002): 269-290. doi: 10.1111/1464-0597.00092.

Bauni, Evasius K., and Ben Obonyo Jarabi. "The Low Acceptability and Use of Condoms within Marriage: Evidence from Nakuru District, Kenya." African Population Studies 18, no. 1(2003): 51-65.

BBC Media Action. "Condom is just another word". Accessed March 19, 2012.

http://www.bbc.co.uk/mediaaction/where_we_work/asia/india/condo
m_condom.html

Bentley, Margaret E., Kai Spratt, Mary E. Shepherd, Raman R. Gangakhedkar, S. Thilikavathi, Robert C. Bollinger, and Sanjay M. Mehendale. "HIV testing and counseling among men attending sexually transmitted disease clinics in Pune, India: changes in condom use and sexual behavior over time." Aids 12, no. 14 (1998): 1869-1877.

Bhattacharya, Gauri. "Sociocultural and behavioral contexts of condom use in heterosexual married couples in India: challenges to the HIV prevention program." Health Education & Behavior 31, no. 1 (2004): 101-117. doi: 10.1177/1090198103259204.

Bond, Virginia, and Paul Dover. "Men, women and the trouble with condoms: problems associated with condom use by migrant workers in rural Zambia." Health transition review (1997): 377-391.

Breakthrough. "Bell Bajaao (Ring the Bell)." Accessed Mar 14 2012.

http://breakthrough.tv/explore/campaign/bell-bajao-ring-the-bell/

Breakthrough. "Is This Justice?" Accessed March 14, 2012.

http://breakthrough.tv/explore/campaign/is-this-justice/

Breakthrough. "Is This Justice?-Summary of Campaign Evaluation." Accessed March 14, 2012.

http://breakthrough.tv/wp/wpcontent/files_mf/1330801847Is_this_4_pger_LoRes.pdf

Breakthrough. "What Kind of Man Are You?"Accessed November 2011.

http://breakthrough.tv/explore/campaign/what-kind-of-man-are-you/

BreakthroughInsights. "Breakthrough's Bell Bajao- A Campaign to Bring Domestic Violence to a Halt." Accessed November 2011.

 http://breakthrough.tv/wp/wp-content/files_mf/1330816837BellBajao_Insight.pdf.

Bryan, Angela D., Jeffrey D. Fisher, and T. Joseph Benziger. "Determinants of HIV risk among Indian truck drivers." Social science & medicine 53, no. 11 (2001): 1413-1426.doi: 10.1016/S0277-9536(00)00435-4.

Bujra, Janet. "Risk and trust: unsafe sex, gender and AIDS in Tanzania." Risk revisited. Edited by Caplan, Pat . London: Pluto Press 2000.

Campbell, Catherine and Yodwa Mzaidume. "How can HIV be prevented in South Africa? A social perspective." BMJ: British Medical Journal 324, no. 7331 (2002): 229-232.

CensusInfo India Dashboard, "Census of India, 2011". Accessed Mar 19, 2012, http://censusindia.gov.in/2011census/censusinfodashboard/index.html

Chandhick, N., B. S. Dhillon, I. Kambo, and N. C. Saxena. "Contraceptive knowledge, practices and utilization of services in the rural areas of India (an ICMR task force study)." Indian Journal of Medical Sciences 57, no. 7 (2003): 303.

Chandrasekaran, Varalakshmi, Karl Krupp, Ruja George, and Purnima Madhivanan. "Determinants of domestic violence among women attending an human immunodeficiency virus voluntary counseling and testing center in Bangalore, India." Indian Journal of Medical Sciences 61, no. 5 (2007): 253-262.doi: 10.4103/0019-5359.32091.

Chankapa, Yalley Dolma, Ranabir Pal, and Dechenla Tsering. "Male behavior toward reproductive responsibilities in Sikkim." Indian journal of community medicine: official publication of Indian Association of Preventive & Social Medicine 35, no. 1 (2010): 40-45. doi: 10.4103/0970-0218.62552.

Chatterjee, N. "AIDS-related information exposure in the mass media and discussion within social networks among married women in Bombay, India." AIDS care 11, no. 4 (1999): 443-446.doi: 10.1080/09540129947820.

Chatterjee, N., and G. M. Hosain. "Perceptions of risk and behaviour change for prevention of HIV among married women in Mumbai, India." Journal of Health, Population, and Nutrition 24, no. 1 (2006): 81-88.

Cohen, Jon. "HIV/AIDS: India's Many Epidemics." Science 304, no.5670 (2004): 504-509.doi: 10.1126/science.304.5670.504.

Cornman, Deborah H., Sarah J. Schmiege, Angela Bryan, T. Joseph Benziger, and Jeffrey D. Fisher. "An information-motivation-behavioral skills (IMB) model-based HIV prevention intervention for truck drivers in India." Social Science & Medicine 64, no. 8 (2007): 1572-1584.doi: 10.1016/j.socscimed.2006.11.011.

Correa, S. and R. Petchesky. Reproductive and sexual Rights: A feminist perspective. In G. Sen, A. Germain and L. C. Chen (eds.) Population Policies Reconsidered: Health, Empowerment and Rights. Harvard School of Public Health. Boston, Massachusetts, 1994.

Dahl, Darren W., Peter R. Darke, Gerald J. Gorn, and Charles B. Weinberg. "Promiscuous or Confident? Attitudinal Ambivalence Toward Condom Purchase1." Journal of Applied Social Psychology 35, no. 4 (2005): 869-887.doi: 10.1111/j.1559-1816.2005.tb02150.x.

Dasgupta, Shamita Das. "Charting the course: An overview of domestic violence in the South Asian community in the United States." Journal of social distress and the homeless 9, no. 3 (2000): 173-185.doi: 10.1023/A:1009403917198.

Davila, Yolanda R. "Hispanic women and AIDS: Gendered risk factors and clinical implications." Issues in mental health nursing 21, no. 6 (2000): 635-646., doi:10.1080/01612840050110326

Davila, Yolanda R. "Influence of abuse on condom negotiation among Mexican-American women involved in abusive relationships." Journal of the Association of Nurses in AIDS Care 13, no. 6 (2002): 46-56.doi: 10.1177/1055329002238025.

240

Davila, Yolanda R., and Margaret H. Brackley. "Mexican and Mexican American women in a battered women's shelter: barriers to condom negotiation for HIV/AIDS prevention." Issues in mental health nursing 20, no. 4 (1999): 333-355. ,doi:10.1080/016128499248529.

Decker, Michele R., George R. Seage III, David Hemenway, Anita Raj, Niranjan Saggurti, Donta Balaiah, and Jay G. Silverman. "Intimate partner violence functions as both a risk marker and risk factor for women's HIV infection: findings from Indian husband-wife dyads." JAIDS Journal of Acquired Immune Deficiency Syndromes 51, no. 5 (2009): 593-600.doi: 10.1097/QAI.0b013e3181a255d6.

Dhingra, Rajni, Sarika Manhas, Nidhi Kohli, and Asiya Mushtaq. "Attitude of Couples towards Family Planning." Journal of Human Ecology 30, no. 1 (2010): 63-70.

Dunkle, Kristin L., Rachel K. Jewkes, Heather C. Brown, Glenda E. Gray, James A. McIntryre, and Siobán D. Harlow. "Gender-based violence, relationship power, and risk of HIV infection in women attending antenatal clinics in South Africa." The Lancet 363, no. 9419 (2004): 1415-1421. doi:10.1016/S0140-6736(04)16098-4.

El-Bassel, N., L. Gilbert, V. Rajah, A. Foleno, and V. Frye. "Fear and violence: raising the HIV stakes." AIDS education and prevention: official publication of the International Society for AIDS Education 12, no. 2 (2000): 154-170.

Ellsberg, M. C., A. Winkvist, R. Peña, and H. Stenlund. "Women's strategic responses to violence in Nicaragua." Journal of Epidemiology and community Health 55, no. 8 (2001): 547-555. doi:10.1136/jech.55.8.547.

Ellsberg, Mary, and Lori Heise. "Bearing witness: ethics in domestic violence research." The Lancet 359, no. 9317 (2002): 1599-1604.

Fayorsey, Charles. "Family planning in Africa; the relevance of gender issues." Developments in Family Planning Policies and Programmes in Africa (1989): 194-229.

Freimuth, Vicki S. "Theoretical foundations of AIDS media campaigns." AIDS: A communication perspective (1992): 91-110.

Frieze, I. H. "Investigating the Causes and Consequences of Marital Rape." Signs 8, no. 3 (1983): 532-553.

Gamson, Joshua. "Rubber wars: Struggles over the condom in the United States." Journal of the History of Sexuality 1, no. 2 (1990): 262-282.

Gangakhedkar, Raman R., Margaret E. Bentley, Anand D. Divekar, Deepak Gadkari, Sanjay M. Mehendale, Mary E. Shepherd, Robert C. Bollinger, and Thomas C. Quinn. "Spread of HIV infection in married monogamous women in India." JAMA: the journal of the American Medical Association 278, no. 23 (1997): 2090-2092.

doi:10.1001/jama.1997.03550230066039.

Garcia-Moreno, Claudia, and Charlotte Watts. "Violence against women: its importance for HIV/AIDS." AIDS 14, suppl. 3 (2000): S253-S265.

Garcia-Moreno, Claudia, Henrica AFM Jansen, Mary Ellsberg, Lori Heise, and Charlotte Watts. WHO multi-country study on women's health and domestic violence against women: initial results on prevalence, health outcomes and women's responses. World Health Organization, 2005.

George, Annie, and Surinder Singh Jaswal. Understanding sexuality: An ethnographic study of poor women in Bombay, India. International Center for Research on Women, 1995.

George, Annie. "Differential perspectives of men and women in Mumbai, India on sexual relations and negotiations within marriage." Reproductive Health Matters 6, no. 12 (1998): 87-96.doi: 10.1016/S0968-8080(98)90011-8.

Ghosh, Jayati, Vandana Wadhwa, and Ezekiel Kalipeni. "Vulnerability to HIV/AIDS among women of reproductive age in the slums of Delhi and Hyderabad, India." Social Science & Medicine 68, no. 4 (2009): 638-642.doi: 10.1016/j.socscimed.2008.11.023.

Ghosh, P., O. A. Arah, A. Talukdar, D. Sur, G. R. Babu, P. Sengupta, and R. Detels. "Factors associated with HIV infection among Indian women." International journal of STD & AIDS 22, no. 3 (2011): 140-145. doi: 10.1258/ijsa.2010.010127.

Go, Vivian F., C. Johnson Sethulakshmi, Margaret E. Bentley, Sudha Sivaram, A. K. Srikrishnan, Suniti Solomon, and David D. Celentano. "When HIV-prevention messages and gender norms clash: the impact of domestic violence on women's HIV risk in slums of Chennai, India." AIDS and Behavior 7, no. 3 (2003): 263-272.

doi: 10.1023/A:1025443719490.

Godbole, Sheela, and Sanjay Mehendale. "HIV/AIDS epidemic in India: risk factors, risk behaviour & strategies for prevention & control." Indian J Med Res 121, no. 4 (2005): 356-368.

Gracia, Enrique, and Juan Herrero. "Acceptability of domestic violence against women in the European Union: A multilevel analysis." Journal of epidemiology and community health 60, no. 2 (2006): 123-129. doi:10.1136/jech.2005.036533.

Gracia, Enrique. "Unreported cases of domestic violence against women: Towards an epidemiology of social silence, tolerance, and inhibition." Journal of epidemiology and community health 58, no. 7 (2004): 536-537. doi:10.1136/jech.2003.019604.

Greene, Jennifer C., Valerie J. Caracelli, and Wendy F. Graham. "Toward a conceptual framework for mixed-method evaluation designs." Educational evaluation and policy analysis 11, no. 3 (1989): 255-274.doi: 10.3102/01623737011003255.

Gupta, Geeta Rao, and Ellen Weiss. "Women's lives and sex: Implications for AIDS prevention." Culture, medicine and psychiatry 17, no. 4 (1993): 399-412.

doi: 10.1007/BF01379307.

Gupta, Geeta Rao. "Gender, sexuality, and HIV/AIDS: The what, the why, and the how." In Plenary Address, XIIIth International AIDS Conference, Durban, South Africa, July, vol. 12, 2000.

Gupta, Geeta Rao. "How men's power over women fuels the HIV epidemic: It limits women's ability to control sexual interactions." BMJ: British Medical Journal 324, no. 7331 (2002): 183-184.

Hassan, Fatma, Laura S. Sadowski, Shrikant I. Bangdiwala, Beatriz Vizcarra, Laurie Ramiro, Cristiane S. De Paula, Isabel AS Bordin, and M. K. Mitra. "Physical intimate partner violence in Chile, Egypt, India and the Philippines." Injury Control and Safety Promotion 11, no. 2 (2004): 111-116.doi: 10.1080/15660970412331292333.

Hawkes, Sarah, and K. G. Santhya. "Diverse realities: sexually transmitted infections and HIV in India." Sexually Transmitted Infections 78, no. suppl 1 (2002): i31-i39. doi:10.1136/sti.78.suppl_1.i31.

Heise LL, Pitanguy J, Germain A, "Violence against women: the hidden health burden." Discussion paper no. 255.Washington DC: World Bank (1994).

Heise, Lori L., and Christopher Elias. "Transforming AIDS prevention to meet women's needs: a focus on developing countries." Social science & medicine 40, no. 7 (1995): 931-943.doi: 10.1016/0277-9536(94)00165-P.

Heise, Lori L., Jacqueline Pitanguy, and Adrienne Germain. "Violence against women: the hidden health burden; Violence against women: the hidden health burden." World Bank Discussion Papers 255 (1994). Washington D.C.: The World Bank.

Helweg-Larsen, Marie, and Barry E. Collins. "The UCLA Multidimensional Condom Attitudes Scale: Documenting the complex determinants of condom use in college students." Health Psychology 13, no. 3 (1994): 224-237.doi: 10.1037/0278-6133.13.3.224.

Holstein, James A., and Jaber F. Gubrium. "The active interview". Vol. 37. Sage Publications, Incorporated, 1995.

http://www.proud2bindian.in/indian-law-judiciary/3747-maharashtra-police-helpline numbers.html

International Clinical Epidemiologists Network (INCLEN). "Domestic Violence in India 3: A Summary Report of a Multi–Site Household Survey." Washington, D.C.: International Centre for Research on Women and Centre for Development and Population Activities 2000.

International Institute for Population Sciences (IIPS) and Macro International. "Domestic Violence." National Family Health Survey (NFHS-3), 2005–06: India Volume I. Mumbai: IIPS (2007).

International Institute for Population Sciences (IIPS) and Macro International. "HIV/AIDS Related Knowledge, Attitudes, and

Behaviour." National Family Health Survey (NFHS-3), 2005–06: India , Volume I. Mumbai: IIPS (2007).

International Institute for Population Sciences (IIPS) and Macro International. "HIV Prevalence."National Family Health Survey (NFHS-3), 2005–06: India Volume I. Mumbai: IIPS (2007).

International Institute for Population Sciences (IIPS) and Macro International. "Family Planning." National Family Health Survey (NFHS-3), 2005–06: India Volume I. Mumbai: IIPS (2007).

International Institute for Population Sciences (IIPS) and Macro International. " National Family Health Survey (NFHS-3), 2005–06: India: Volume I." Mumbai: IIPS 2007. pp. 387

International Organizations of Medical Sciences (CIOMS). "International Ethical Guidelines for Biomedical research." World Health Organization (WHO), Geneva, 2002. Accessed May 2008, http://www.cioms.ch/publications/layout_guide2002.pdf

Jatania, Prachi. "Married and cheating? Balbir Pasha's watching you." The Indian Express, November 18, 2004. Accessed Mar 20, 2012.

http://www.indianexpress.com/oldStory/59099/

Jejeebhoy, Shireen J. "Associations between wife-beating and fetal and infant death: impressions from a survey in rural India." Studies in family planning 29, no.3 (1998): 300-308.

Jejeebhoy, Shireen J., and Rebecca J. Cook. "State accountability for wife-beating: the indian challenge." The Lancet 349 (1997): S10-S12.

Jeyaseelan, Lakshman, Shuba Kumar, Nithya Neelakantan, Abraham Peedicayil, Rajamohanam Pillai, and Nata Duvvury. "Physical spousal violence against women in India: some risk factors." Journal of biosocial science 39, no. 5 (2007): 657-670.doi: 10.1017/S0021932007001836.

Kalichman, Seth C., Ernestine A. Williams, Charsey Cherry, Lisa Belcher, and Dena Nachimson. "Sexual coercion, domestic violence, and negotiating condom use among low-income African American women." Journal of Women's Health 7, no. 3 (1998): 371-378. doi:10.1089/jwh.1998.7.371.

Karanja, Lisa. Just Die Quietly. Domestic Violence and Women's Vulnerability to HIV in Uganda." New York: HRW Reports 15, no. 15A (2003).

Kaur, Ravneet, and Suneela Garg. "Addressing domestic violence against women: An unfinished agenda." Indian Journal of Community Medicine: Official Publication of Indian Association of Preventive & Social Medicine 33, no. 2 (2008): 73-76. doi: 10.4103/0970-0218.40871.

Kaye, Dan K. "Gender inequality and domestic violence: implications for human immunodeficiency virus (HIV) prevention." African health sciences 4, no. 1 (2004): 67-70.

Khan M E, Patel Bella C. "Male Involvement in Family Planning - A KABP Study of Agra District Uttar Pradesh Final Report." New Delhi: Population Council, 1997.

Khan, M. E. and Patel, B. C. "Level of Unwanted Pregnancies and Its Consequences."Paper presented in IUSSP Seminar on Socio-cultural and Political Aspects of Abortion from an Anthropological Perspective, March 25-28, 1996.

Khan, M. E., John W. Townsend, Ranjana Sinha, and Seema Lakhanpal. "Sexual violence within marriage." New Delhi: Centre for Operations Research and Training (CORT)- Working Paper no. 12.,1996.

Kishor Sunita and Gupta kamla. "Gender Equality and Women's Empowerment in India." National Family Health Survey (NFHS-3), India, 2005-06 (2009). Mumbai: International Institute for Population Sciences (2009); Calverton, Maryland, USA: ICF Macro.

Kishor Sunita and Gupta kamla. "Gender Relations: Norms and Attitudes." In   Gender Equality and Women's Empowerment in India. National Family Health Survey (NFHS-3), India, 2005-06. Mumbai: International Institute for Population Sciences (2009); Calverton, Maryland, USA: ICF Macro.

Kishor, Sunita, and Kiersten Johnson. "Profiling domestic violence: a multi-country study." MEASURE DHS +, ORC Macro, 2004.

Koenig, Michael A., Rob Stephenson, Saifuddin Ahmed, Shireen J. Jejeebhoy, and Jacquelyn Campbell. "Individual and contextual determinants of domestic violence in North India." Journal Information 96, no. 1 (2006):132-138., doi:10.2105/AJPH.2004.050872.

Koenig, Michael A., Tom Lutalo, Feng Zhao, Fred Nalugoda, Fred Wabwire-Mangen, Noah Kiwanuka, Jennifer Wagman, David Serwadda, Maria Wawer, and Ron Gray. "Domestic violence in rural Uganda: evidence from a community-based study." Bulletin of the World Health Organization 81, no. 1 (2003): 53-60.

Koenig, Michael A., Tom Lutalo, Feng Zhao, Fred Nalugoda, Noah Kiwanuka, Fred Wabwire-Mangen, Godfrey Kigozi et al. "Coercive sex in rural Uganda: prevalence and associated risk factors." Social Science & Medicine 58, no. 4 (2004): 787-798., doi: 10.1016/S0277-9536(03)00244-2.

Krug, Etienne G., James A. Mercy, Linda L. Dahlberg, and Anthony B. Zwi. "The world report on violence and health." The lancet 360, no. 9339 (2002): 1083-1088.doi: 10.1016/S0140-6736(02)11133-0.

Kumar, Satish, S. Gupta, George Abraham, J. Jeyaranjan, S. Daga Anandhi, Abdul Rahman, Nata Duvvury, Madhabika Nayak, and Keera Allendorf. "Men, Masculinity and Domestic Violence in India. Summary Report of Four Studies." Washington, D.C.: International Centre for Research on Women, 2002.

Lal, Shiv. "Current status of AIDS and HIV infection in India." Journal of the Indian Medical Association 92, no. 1 (1994): 3-4.

Lawyers Collective and The International Center for Research on Women. "Staying Alive: Fourth Monitoring & Evaluation Report on the Protection of Women from Domestic Violence Act, 2005", 2010. Accessed November 2011.

http://www.unwomensouthasia.org/assets/LCWRI-4th-PWDVA-ME-Report-2010-Staying-Alive3.pdf

Lawyers Collective Women's Rights Initiative (LCWRI). "Staying Alive:5th Monitoring and Evaluation Report on the Protection of Women from Domestic Violence Act, 2005." New Delhi, 2012.

Lawyers Collective. "Protection of Women against Domestic Violence Act 2005," Accessed March 18, 2012.

http://www.lawyerscollective.org/files/protection_of_women_from_domestic_violence_act_2005.pdf

Lee, Mo Yee, and Phyllis FM Law. "Perception of sexual violence against women in Asian American communities." Journal of ethnic and cultural diversity in social work 10, no. 2 (2001): 3-25. doi:10.1300/J051v10n02_02

Lee, Mo Yee, and Phyllis FM Law. "Perception of sexual violence against women in Asian American communities." Journal of ethnic and cultural diversity in social work 10, no. 2 (2001): 3-25. doi: 10.1300/J051v10n02_02.

Lupton, Deborah. "The condom in the age of AIDS: Newly respectable or still a dirty word? A discourse analysis." Qualitative

251

Health Research 4, no. 3 (1994): 304-320. doi: 10.1177/104973239400400304

Maharaj, Pranitha, and John Cleland. "Condom Use Within Marital and Cohabiting Partnerships in KwaZulu-Natal, South Africa." Studies in Family Planning 35, no. 2 (2004): 116-124. doi: 10.1111/j.1728-4465.2004.00013.x

Maliki, Agnes Ebi, Monday Ehikioya Omohan, and Ekanem Anwana Uwe. "HIV/AIDS and Use of Condom: The Role of Counsellors." Journal of Students, Tribes and Tribals 4, no.2 (2006):151-155.

Maman, Suzanne, Jacquelyn Campbell, Michael D. Sweat, and Andrea C. Gielen. "The intersections of HIV and violence: directions for future research and interventions." Social science & medicine 50, no. 4 (2000): 459-478. doi: 10.1016/S0277-9536(99)00270-1.

Martin, Elaine K., Casey T. Taft, and Patricia A. Resick. "A review of marital rape." Aggression and Violent Behavior 12, no. 3 (2007): 329-347.doi: 10.1016/j.avb.2006.10.003.

Martin, Sandra L., Amy Ong Tsui, Kuhu Maitra, and Ruth Marinshaw. "Domestic violence in northern India." American Journal of Epidemiology 150, no. 4 (1999): 417-426.

Martin, Sandra L., and Sian Curtis. "Gender-based violence and HIV/AIDS: recognising links and acting on evidence." The Lancet 363, no. 9419 (2004): 1410-1411. doi: 10.1016/S0140-6736(04)16133-3

Martin, Sandra L., Brian Kilgallen, Amy Ong Tsui, Kuhu Maitra, Kaushalendra Kumar Singh, and Lawrence L. Kupper. "Sexual behaviors and reproductive health outcomes : Associations with wife abuse in India." JAMA: the journal of the American Medical Association 282, no. 20 (1999): 1967-1972. doi:10.1001/jama.282.20.1967.

Martin, Sandra L., Kathryn E. Moracco, Julian Garro, Amy Ong Tsui, Lawrence L. Kupper, Jennifer L. Chase, and Jacquelyn C. Campbell. "Domestic violence across generations: findings from northern India." International Journal of Epidemiology 31, no. 3 (2002): 560-572. doi: 10.1093/ije/31.3.560.

Mbizvo, Michael T., and M. T. Bassett. "Reproductive health and AIDS prevention in sub-Saharan Africa: the case for increased male participation." Health Policy and Planning 11, no. 1 (1996): 84-92. doi: 10.1093/heapol/11.1.84.

MEASURE DHS. "Domestic violence module." DHS Questionnaires and Manuals, September 22, 2005. Accessed May 2008.

http://www.measuredhs.com/pubs/pdf/DHSQMP/DHS5_Module_Domestic_Violence.pdf

MEASURE DHS. "Women's status module." DHS Questionnaires and Manuals, September 22, 2005. Accessed May 2008.

http://www.measuredhs.com/pubs/pdf/DHSQMP/DHS5_Module_Womens_Status_Sept05.pdf.

Mehta, Shruti H., Amita Gupta, Seema Sahay, Sheela V. Godbole, Smita N. Joshi, Steven J. Reynolds, David D. Celentano, Arun Risbud, Sanjay M. Mehendale, and Robert C. Bollinger. "High HIV prevalence among a high-risk subgroup of women attending sexually transmitted infection clinics in Pune, India." JAIDS Journal of Acquired Immune Deficiency Syndromes 41, no. 1 (2006): 75-80.

Miles, Matthew B., and A. Michael Huberman. "Qualitative data analysis: An expanded sourcebook." Sage Publications, Incorporated, 1994.

National AIDS Control Organisation (Ministry of Health & Family Welfare, Government of India), "Epidemiological Situation and Projections", in Strategy and Implementation Plan – National AIDS Control Programme– Phase III (2006-2011), 2006

National AIDS Control Organization (NACO), "Information, Education & Communication and Mainstreaming", in Annual Report 2010-11: 24, New Delhi, Ministry of Health and Family Welfare, Government of India

National AIDS Control Organization (NACO), National Behavioural Surveillance Survey (BSS), 2006, New Delhi, Ministry of Health and Family Welfare, Government of India.

National AIDS Control Organization (NACO), UNGASS India report: Progress report on the Declaration of Commitment on HIV/AIDS, United Nations General Assembly Special Session on HIV/AIDS, 2005, New Delhi: NACO, Ministry of Health and Family Welfare, Government of India.

National AIDS Control Organization (NACO), UNGASS India report: Progress report on the Declaration of Commitment on HIV/AIDS, United Nations General Assembly Special Session on HIV/AIDS, 2010, New Delhi: NACO, Ministry of Health and Family Welfare, Government of India.

National AIDS Control Organization (NACO). " UNGASS India report: Progress report on the Declaration of Commitment on HIV/AIDS." United Nations General Assembly Special Session on HIV/AIDS. NACO, Ministry of Health and Family Welfare, Government of India. New Delhi, 2005. Accessed March 19, 2012.

http://data.unaids.org/pub/Report/2006/2006_country_progress_repo rt_india_en.pdf

National AIDS Control Organization (NACO). "Annual Report-2010-11." Department of AIDS Control , NACO, Ministry of Health and Family Welfare, Government of India. New Delhi, March 15, 2011. Accessed Dec 2011.

http://www.nacoonline.org/upload/REPORTS/NACO%20Annual%2 0Report%202010-11.pdf

National AIDS Control Organization (NACO). "Awareness Raising (Services for Prevention)-NACP-III." accessed Mar 18, 2012.,

http://www.nacoonline.org/National_AIDS_Control_Program/Servic es_for_Prevention/Awareness_Raising/

Newmann, S., P. Sarin, N. Kumarasamy, E. Amalraj, M. Rogers, P. Madhivanan, T. Flanigan, S. Cu-Uvin, S. McGarvey, K. Mayer and S. Solomon. "Marriage, monogamy and HIV: a profile of HIV-infected women in south India." International journal of STD & AIDS 11, no. 4 (2000): 250-253. doi: 10.1258/0956462001915796.

Nichols, Margaret. "Women and Acquired Immunodeficiency Syndrome: Issues for Prevention." Voeller, Bruce, Machover Reiniscch, June and Gottlieb, Michael. AIDS and Sex: An Integrated Biomedical and Biobehavioural Approach (1990).

Njovana, Eunice, and Charlotte Watts. "Gender violence in Zimbabwe: a need for collaborative action." Reproductive health matters 4, no. 7 (1996): 46-55. doi: 10.1016/S0968-8080(96)90005-1.

Nussbaum, Martha, and Jonathan Glover, eds. Women, culture, and development: A study of human capabilities. Oxford University Press, USA, 1996.

OCDE. Economic Survey of India 2011. Accessed March 2012.

http://www.oecd.org/india/economicsurveyofindia2011.htm

Operations Research Group. Family Planning Practices in India: Third All India Family Planning Survey. Monograph, ORG, Baroda, 1990.

Östlin, Piroska, Elizabeth Eckermann, Udaya Shankar Mishra, Mwansa Nkowane, and Eva Wallstam. "Gender and health promotion: A multisectoral policy approach." Health Promotion

International 21, no. suppl 1 (2006): 25-35. doi: 10.1093/heapro/dal048.

Ouattara, Mariam, Purna Sen, and Marilyn Thomson. "Forced marriage, forced sex: the perils of childhood for girls." Gender & Development 6, no. 3 (1998): 27-33.doi: 10.1080/741922829.

Padma Rama G. "Gendered norms: detrimental to knowledge and increases HIV risk." Paper presented at the XVI International AIDS Conference: Abstract no. CDD0043. Toronto, Ontario, 13–18 August 2006.

Pallikadavath, Saseendran, and R. William Stones. "Women's reproductive health security and HIV/AIDS in India." Economic and Political Weekly (2003): 4173-4181.

Panchanadeswaran, Subadra, and Catherine Koverola. "The voices of battered women in India." Violence Against Women 11, no. 6 (2005): 736-758. doi: 10.1177/1077801205276088.

Panchanadeswaran, Subadra, Sethulakshmi C. Johnson, Vivian F. Go, A. K. Srikrishnan, Sudha Sivaram, Suniti Solomon, Margaret E. Bentley, and David Celentano. "Using the theory of gender and power to examine experiences of partner violence, sexual negotiation, and risk of HIV/AIDS among economically disadvantaged women in southern India." Journal of Aggression, Maltreatment & Trauma 15, no. 3-4 (2007): 155-178. doi: 10.1080/10926770802097327.

Panda, Samiran, M. Suresh Kumar, S. Lokabiraman, K. Jayashree, M. C. Satagopan, Suniti Solomon, Usha Anand Rao, Rangaiyan Gurumurthy, Flessenkaemper Sabine, Grosskurth Heiner, and Gupte, Mohan. "Risk factors for HIV infection in injection drug users and evidence for onward transmission of HIV to their sexual partners in Chennai, India." JAIDS Journal of Acquired Immune Deficiency Syndromes 39, no. 1 (2005): 9-15.doi: 10.1097/01.qai.0000160713.94203.9b.

Pande, Rohini Prabha, Tina Y. Falle, Sujit Rathod, Jeffrey Edmeades, and Suneeta Krishnan. "'If your husband calls, you have to go': understanding sexual agency among young married women in urban South India." Sexual Health 8, no. 1 (2011): 102-109.doi: 10.1071/SH10025.

Perkins, Jessica M., Kashif T. Khan, and S. V. Subramanian. "Patterns and distribution of HIV among adult men and women in India." PloS one 4, no. 5 (2009): e5648. doi:10.1371/journal.pone.0005648.

Piotrow, Phyllis T., D. Lawrence Kincaid, Michelle J. Hindin, Cheryl L. Lettenmaier, Innocent Kuseka, Terry Silberman, Alex Zinanga et al. "Changing men's attitudes and behavior: the Zimbabwe Male Motivation Project." Studies in Family Planning 23, no. 6 (1992): 365-375.doi: 10.2307/1966894.

Plummer, Mary L., Daniel Wight, Joyce Wamoyi, Gerry Mshana, Richard J. Hayes, and David A. Ross. "Farming with your hoe in a sack: Condom attitudes, access, and use in rural Tanzania." Studies in family planning 37, no. 1 (2006): 29-40.doi: 10.1111/j.1728-4465.2006.00081.x.

Prasad, Shally. "Medicolegal response to violence against women in India." Violence Against Women 5, no. 5 (1999): 478-506.doi: 10.1177/10778019922181338.

Pulerwitz, Julie, Steven L. Gortmaker, and William DeJong. "Measuring sexual relationship power in HIV/STD research." Sex Roles 42, no. 7 (2000): 637-660.doi: 10.1023/A:1007051506972.

Quigley, Maria A., Dilys Morgan, Samuel S. Malamba, Billy Mayanja, Martin J. Okongo, Lucy M. Carpenter, and James A. Whitworth. "Case-control study of risk factors for incident HIV infection in rural Uganda." JAIDS Journal of Acquired Immune Deficiency Syndromes 23, no. 5 (2000): 418-425.

Rao, Vijayendra. "Wife-beating in rural South India: a qualitative and econometric analysis." Social science & medicine 44, no. 8 (1997): 1169-1180.doi: 10.1016/S0277-9536(96)00252-3

Reid, Elizabeth, and Michael Bailey. "Young Women: Silence, Susceptibility and the HIV Epidemic." Issue paper no. 12. New York: HIV and Development Programme, United Nations Development Programme 1993.

Reid, Elizabeth, and Michael Bailey. Young women: silence, susceptibility and the HIV epidemic. United Nations Development Programme, 1992.

Ries Al and Trout J. "Marketing Warfare." New York: McGraw-Hill.1986.

Robey, B., and M. Drennan. "Male participation in reproductive health." Network 18, no. 3 (1998): 11.

Rocca, Corinne H., Sujit Rathod, Tina Falle, Rohini P. Pande, and Suneeta Krishnan. "Challenging assumptions about women's empowerment: social and economic resources and domestic violence among young married women in urban South India." International Journal of Epidemiology 38, no. 2 (2009): 577-585. doi: 10.1093/ije/dyn226

Roger , E M. Diffusion of innovations (5th ed.).New York: The Free Press, 2003.

Rossman, Gretchen B., and Bruce L. Wilson. "Numbers and words revisited: Being "shamelessly eclectic"." Quality & Quantity 28, no. 3 (1994): 315-327.

Roth, Joseph, Satya P. Krishnan, and Emily Bunch. "Barriers to condom use: results from a study in Mumbai (Bombay), India." AIDS Education and Prevention 13, no. 1 (2001): 65-77. doi: 10.1521/aeap.13.1.65.18925.

Sacco, William P., Richard L. Rickman, Karla Thompson, and Brian Levine. "Gender differences in AIDS-relevant condom attitudes and condom use." AIDS Education and Prevention Vol. 5(4), 1993, 311-326.

Saluja, N., S. Sharma, S. Choudhary, D. R. Gaur, and S. M. Pandey. "Contraceptive Knowledge, Attitude and Practice Among Eligible Couples of Rural Haryana." The Internet Journal of Health 12, no. 1 (2011). doi: 10.5580/156e.

Sarkar, N. N. "Barriers to condom use." European J. of Contraception and Reproductive Healthcare 13, no. 2 (2008): 114-122. doi:10.1080/13625180802011302.

Schensul, Stephen L., Abdelwahed Mekki-Berrada, Bonnie K. Nastasi, Rajendra Singh, Joseph A. Burleson, and Martha Bojko. "Men's extramarital sex, marital relationships and sexual risk in urban poor communities in India." Journal of Urban Health 83, no. 4 (2006): 614-624.doi: 10.1007/s11524-006-9076-z.

Sen, Gita, and Srilatha Batliwala. "Empowering women for reproductive rights." Women's empowerment and demographic processes (2000): 15-36.,

http://www.dnaindia.com/mumbai/report_helpline-103-will-now-be-for-all-women-in-maharashtra_1355417.

Sharma, Somendra. "Helpline 103 will now be for all women in Maharashtra." Daily News & Analysis (DNA), March 5, 2010. Accessed March 12, 2011.

Sharma, V., S. Dave, A. Sharma, and P. Chauhan. "Condoms: mis-use= non-use. The condom equation in Gujarat, India." Aids Care 9, no. 6 (1997): 707-714.doi: 10.1080/713613231.

Sherrif of Mumbai. "1298 Women's Helpline." Accessed March 12, 2011.

http://www.sheriffofmumbai.com/1298.html

Shrotri, A., A. V. Shankar, S. Sutar, A. Joshi, N. Suryawanshi, H. Pisal, K. E. Bharucha, M. A. Phadke, R. C. Bollinger, and J. Sastry. "Awareness of HIV/AIDS and household environment of pregnant women in Pune, India." International journal of STD & AIDS 14, no. 12 (2003): 835-839.doi: 10.1258/095646203322556183.

Silverman, Jay G., Michele R. Decker, Niranjan Saggurti, Donta Balaiah, and Anita Raj. "Intimate partner violence and HIV infection among married Indian women." JAMA: the journal of the American Medical Association 300, no. 6 (2008): 703-710. doi:10.1001/jama.300.6.703.

Sinding, Steven W. "Does' CNN'(condoms, needles and negotiation) work better than'ABC'(abstinence, being faithful and condom use) in attacking the AIDS epidemic?." International Family Planning Perspectives (2005): 38-40.

Singhal, Arvind, and Everett M. Rogers. Entertainment-education: A communication strategy for social change. Lawrence Erlbaum Associates Publishers, 1999.

Sivaram, Sudha, Sethulakshmi Johnson, Margaret E. Bentley, Vivian F. Go, Carl Latkin, A. K. Srikrishnan, David D. Celentano, and Suniti Solomon. "Sexual health promotion in Chennai, India: key role of communication among social networks." Health Promotion International 20, no. 4 (2005): 327-333. doi: 10.1093/heapro/dai012.

Solomon, Sunil S., Aylur K. Srikrishnan, David D. Celentano, Sethulakshmi C. Johnson, Canjeevaram K. Vasudevan, Kailapuri G. Murugavel, Santhanam Anand, M. Suresh Kumar, Suniti Solomon, and Shruti H. Mehta. "The intersection between sex and drugs: a cross-sectional study among the spouses of injection drug users in Chennai, India." BMC public health 11, no. 1 (2011): 39. doi:10.1186/1471-2458-11-39.

Solomon, Sunil S., Shruti H. Mehta, Amanda Latimore, Aylur K. Srikrishnan, and David D. Celentano. "The impact of HIV and high-risk behaviours on the wives of married men who have sex with men and injection drug users: implications for HIV prevention." Journal of the International AIDS Society 13, no. Suppl 2 (2010): S7. doi:10.1186/1758-2652-13-S2-S7.

Solomon, Suniti, N. Kumarasamy, A. K. Ganesh, and R. Edwin Amalraj. "Prevalence and risk factors of HIV-1 and HIV-2 infection in urban and rural areas in Tamil Nadu, India." International journal of STD & AIDS 9, no. 2 (1998): 98-103. doi: 10.1258/0956462981921756.

Solomon, Suniti. "Stopping HIV Infection Before It Begins in Women." Paper presented at 10th Conf Retroviruses Opportunistic Infections, Boston, MA, USA, February 10-14, 2003.

Sri Krishnan, A. K., Ellen Hendriksen, Snigda Vallabhaneni, Sethu L. Johnson, Sudha Raminani, N. Kumarasamy, Jeremy Hobsen,

Suniti Solomon, Kenneth H. Mayer, and Steven A. Safren. "Sexual behaviors of individuals with HIV living in South India: A qualitative study." AIDS Education & Prevention 19, no. 4 (2007): 334-345.

Stephenson, Rob, Michael A. Koenig, and Saifuddin Ahmed. "Domestic violence and symptoms of gynecologic morbidity among women in North India." International Family Planning Perspectives 32, no. 4 (2006): 201-208.

Swan, Holly, and Daniel J. O'Connell. "The impact of intimate partner violence on women's condom negotiation efficacy." Journal of Interpersonal Violence 27, no. 4 (2012): 775-792.doi: 10.1177/0886260511423240.

Terefe, Almaz, and Charles P. Larson. "Modern contraception use in Ethiopia: Does involving husbands make a difference?." American Journal of Public Health 83, no. 11 (1993): 1567-1571.doi: 10.2105/AJPH.83.11.1567.

The Economist. "Hitting Women." The Economist online, March 8, 2012. Accessed March 12, 2012.
http://www.economist.com/blogs/graphicdetail/2012/03/daily-chart-6.

The Indian Express. "Courting trouble", December 07, 2008. Accessed March 18, 2012.
http://www.indianexpress.com/news/courting-trouble/395318/0.

The Times Of India Mumbai, "Soon, you can call 103 for help from any place in state." March 5, 2010. Accessed March 12, 2011.

http://epaper.timesofindia.com/Repository/ml.asp?Ref=VE9JTS8yM DEwLzAzLzA1I0FyMDA3MDQ=&Mode=HTML&Locale=english -skin-custom.

UN General Assembly. "A/RES/48/104 - Declaration on the Elimination of Violence against Women." 85th plenary meeting, December 20, 1993. Accessed March 18, 2012., http://www.un.org/documents/ga/res/48/a48r104.htm.

UNAIDS. "Joint UN Support Plan for HIV and AIDS India 2007-2011." Delhi, India, 2007.

UNGASS. "Country progress Report – India: Progress report on the Declaration of Commitment on HIV/AIDS." United Nations General Assembly Special Session on HIV/AIDS, Mar 31, 2010. Accessed March 19, 2012.

http://data.unaids.org/pub/Report/2010/india_2010_country_progress _report_en.pdf

Unicef and Innocenti Research Center." Domestic Violence against Women and Girls. Innocenti Digest 6 (2000).

UNICEF, "Attitude towards Wife-beating." Accessed January 2012.

http://www.childinfo.org/attitudes_data.php.

United Nations Report of the Fourth World Conference on Women, Beijing 4-15 September 1995. United Nations: New York, 1995.

United Nations Economic and Social Council. "E/CN.4/1996/53/Add.2- A framework for model legislation on domestic violence." 52nd session of Commission on Human Rights, February 2, 1996. Accessed March 18, 2012.

http://www.unhchr.ch/Huridocda/Huridoca.nsf/0/0a7aa1c3f8de6f9a8 02566d700530914

United Nations General Assembly. "A/RES/48/104 - Declaration on the Elimination of Violence against Women." 85th plenary meeting, December 20, 1993. Accessed March 12, 2012. http://www.un.org/documents/ga/res/48/a48r104.htm

United Nations. Population and Development: Programme of Action Adopted at the International Conference on Population and Development: Cairo 5-13 September 1994. Department for Economic and Social Information and Policy Analysis, United Nations, 1995.

United States Agency for International Development (USAID). "Balbir Pasha Stirs Protection Talk-case study." Accessed December 2012.

 http://transition.usaid.gov/stories/india/cs_india_aids.html

Varma, Deepthi S., Prabha S. Chandra, Catina Callahan, Wendy Reich, and Linda B. Cottler. "Perceptions of HIV risk among monogamous wives of alcoholic men in South India: A qualitative study." Journal of Women's Health 19, no. 4 (2010): 815-821. doi:10.1089/jwh.2008.0884.

Verma, Ravi K., and Martine Collumbien. "Wife beating and the link with poor sexual health and risk behavior among men in urban slums in India." Journal of Comparative Family Studies 34, no. 1 (2003): 61-74.

Verma, Ravi K., Julie Pulerwitz, Vaishali Mahendra, Sujata Khandekar, Gary Barker, P. Fulpagare, and S.K. Singh. " Shifting support for inequitable gender norms among young Indian men to reduce HIV risk and partner violence." Horizons Research Summary. New Delhi: Population Council, 2006.

Vivian F. Go, Sethulakshmi C. Johnson, Margaret E. Bentley, Sudha Sivaram, A. K. Srikrishnan, David D. Celentano, and Suniti Solomon. "Crossing the threshold: engendered definitions of socially acceptable domestic violence in Chennai, India." Culture, health & sexuality 5, no. 5 (2003): 393-408.doi: 10.1080/136910501164119

Waldner, Lisa K., Linda Vaden-Goad, and Anjoo Sikka. "Sexual coercion in India: An exploratory analysis using demographic variables." Archives of Sexual Behavior 28, no. 6 (1999): 523-538.doi: 10.1023/A:1018717216774.

Weiss, Ellen, Daniel Whelan, and Geeta Rao Gupta. "Gender, sexuality and HIV: making a difference in the lives of young women in developing countries." Sexual and Relationship Therapy 15, no. 3 (2000): 233-245.doi: 10.1080/14681990050109836.

Weiss, Helen A., Vikram Patel, Beryl West, Rosanna W. Peeling, Betty R. Kirkwood, and David Mabey. "Spousal sexual violence and poverty are risk factors for sexually transmitted infections in women: a longitudinal study of women in Goa, India." Sexually transmitted infections 84, no. 2 (2008): 133-139., doi:10.1136/sti.2007.026039.

Wingood, Gina M., and Ralph J. DiClemente. "Partner influences and gender-related factors associated with noncondom use among young adult African American women." American Journal of Community Psychology 26, no. 1 (1998): 29-51.doi: 10.1023/A:1021830023545.

Wingood, Gina M., and Ralph J. DiClemente. "The effects of an abusive primary partner on the condom use and sexual negotiation practices of African-American women." American Journal of Public Health 87, no. 6 (1997): 1016-1018. doi: 10.2105/AJPH.87.6.1016.

World Health Organization, "Putting women first: Ethical and safety recommendation for research on domestic violence against women." WHO/FCH/GWH/01.1. Geneva, 2001. Accessed May 2008. http://www.who.int/gender/violence/womenfirtseng.pdf.

Yadav, Kapil, Bir Singh, and Kiran Goswami. "Agreement and concordance regarding reproductive intentions and contraception between husbands and wives in rural Ballabgarh, India." Indian Journal of Community Medicine: Official Publication of Indian Association of Preventive & Social Medicine 35, no. 1 (2010): 19-23. doi: 10.4103/0970-0218.62548.

Zierler, Sally. "Hitting hard: HIV and violence." The gender politics of HIV/AIDS in women. Perspectives on the pandemic in the United States (1997): 207-221.